90 Days to Desperation

By: Josh Howard

Hoffman and Co. Publishing

HoffmanCoPublishing.com

My lips will glorify You because Your faithful love is better than life. So I will praise You as long as I live; at Your name, I will lift up my hands.

Psalms 63:3-4 HCSB

If you had the chance to have the best life imaginable, anything you wanted when you wanted it, all the money you could dream, perfect relationships, never have to work a day, etc. but it was a life without God, would you take it? The answer should be a quick and resounding no. And yet we are so prone to walk away from the presence of our father for things far inferior to the life mentioned above. Why? Why would we choose that which is wasting away over the eternal? Why would we choose earthly pleasure over that which is far better than life? Are you doing that today? Have you walked away from the God who's love, and kindness are greater than the bearing of your heart for things which will not last? Lift your hands and open your lips to sing praises only to God today. Choose to cling to the One who is better than the best life you could ever imagine. Because a relationship with God truly is better than life. The salvation brought by the blood of Jesus is greater than the breath in your lungs. Thank God for His greatness today. Thank God for His love which is far better than anything we could attain in this life. A wonderful life without God ought to be the most terrible thing you could imagine. You could have everything, and if you didn't have Jesus it would be nothing. And you could have nothing, but if you have Jesus you have everything.

Prayer:

Lord lead me over these next 90 days into a complete desperation for you. Help me to want nothing if you are not in it. Help me Lord, not to pray for more unless it is more of you. Lord I know that, without you, I have nothing. Create in me a need to be closer to you each, and every day.

Amen.

A man who endures trials is blessed, because when he passes the test he will receive the crown of life that God has promised to those who love Him.

James 1:12 HCSB

Setbacks. Setbacks are a guarantee in this life. Sometimes they're our own fault, and sometimes they are struggles outside of our control, but you will have setbacks. But the setbacks don't determine who you are, what you do with them does. In this life you're guaranteed to get sick, you're at least going to catch a cold at some point. That kind of setback can be a pain. You miss work or church, or you don't go to the gym for a few days so you can get better. But you don't just quit after you do get better right? No, you go back to work ready to make up what you've missed. You jump back in the gym, energized, because you can't stand the feeling of getting nothing done. Most people don't let a setback like a nasty cold keep them down for very long. So why do we do that with sin? I've seen so many people fall into sin and decide that, since they already messed up, they may as well stay there. Some stay for days, some for years, and some stay for a lifetime. But why? Why do we quit when we fall prey to our own flesh? When you get a cold you don't just say, "well this is who I am now". Right!? Because it's a sickness. You take medicine, you get better, and you get back to work. Treat sin the same way you would that nasty cold. Run to the one cure for the sickness of the flesh, Jesus. Let Him beat it and then get up and move forward. James says the one who endures trials is blessed, not the one who stays in them. Whatever trial you're in today, self-made or out of your control, let Jesus be the cure. And then get up and get back to work. Your setbacks don't define you, but what you do with them will.

Prayer:

Lord lead me. God search my heart. Reveal to me the setbacks that I have allowed myself to stay in and draw me out of the mire of my own fleshly desires. God I commit to you that, though I will fall, I will turn my eyes to you and refuse to allow my setbacks to define my life.

Amen.

Do not be conformed to this age, but be transformed by the renewing of your mind, so that you may discern what is the good, pleasing, and perfect will of God.

Romans 12:2 HCSB

Are you affecting change, or succumbing to it? Jesus didn't just die so that you could go to heaven, He died in order to change your heart to look more like His. And that change must bleed from you into the world around you. Take a look at your life. Are you changing the world around you? Or is the world around you changing you? Each day you must strive to look more and more like Jesus, and less and less like the world. The world doesn't see Jesus in you when you look just like them, they see Jesus in you when you look like Him. Don't be conformed to the world. Sin is wrong. Integrity and righteousness are to be sought after and worked for. Have you let the world shape you? Are you walking farther from the Lord and looking more like the world? Have you begun to feel less pain over the sin in your life? If so, look to Jesus. Train your heart to look more like Him. Dive into His word and be overcome by it! And fall to your knees and ask Him to transform you to His image. We must look like Jesus, because that is the only way the world will see Him in us.

Prayer:

Lord make me more like your son. Lead me not to be changed by this world, but to affect change in this world through you. God, I pray that my heart and mind would be transformed by you daily. Teach me to surrender to your Son and not to the deceit of this world. I pray Lord that I would look more and more like Jesus until He is all that the world sees when they look at me.

Amen.

Take delight in the Lord, and He will give you your heart's desires.

Psalms 37:4 HCSB

I love this verse. It's short, it's sweet, and it's deeper than the Pacific Ocean. This tiny little verse gives us great insight into how drastically the love of God changes our hearts. When you begin to habitually take delight in the Lord your heart begins to change to look more like His. While it's easy to take this verse and twist it to mean that if we love God, we can have anything we want here on Earth, the actual promise is so much better. When you delight in the Lord, and your heart begins to look more like His, your hearts desires begin to line up with His. Do you see how awesome that is?! The will of the Lord will always be done, His desires will always be carried out. He has no need for you to want what He wants, He's going to get it anyways. He has no need for His will to be your will, it's going to be done anyways. But He WANTS you to be a part of His will. He wants you to be a part of His desires. God wants YOU! And when you delight yourself in Him you get to be a part of His will. When God's desires become your desires, everything this world could offer seems so minute. It pales in comparison. The God of the universe wants to change your heart to look like His, and all you need to do is begin to fall in love with Him. Delight yourself in His word. Delight yourself in His son. Delight yourself in His tender love and mercy. Delight yourself in God and your heart will always be full.

Prayer:

Lord change my heart. I pray that I would not be happy in this life unless I am happy in you. God, thank you for wanting me! Help me to want more of you, more of your presence, more of your love, and more of your Son. God, fill me with you so that your love flows from me into the world around me.

Amen

He spoke these words by the treasury, while teaching in the temple complex. But no one seized Him, because His hour had not come.

John 8:20 HCSB

I love these little nuggets in the gospels. Jesus came to this Earth to be killed as the perfect sacrifice for our sins, but His time here and His death were always within His control. So many times, the Pharisees wanted to grab Jesus and take Him to be executed. So many times, people wished to do Him harm because of the claims of deity that He made. But they couldn't, because Jesus died on the cross for our sins when it was time, and not one moment before. No one took the life of Jesus, He laid it down for you. The Bible says that He could have called down legions of angels to pull Him down from the cross and wipe out all who had done Him harm, and I'm willing to bet those angels stood by to do just that. But He didn't. He went into the garden to pray for you. He walked this Earth for 33 years to set the example for you. And He went to the cross to rescue you. All on His own accord and according to the will of God. Jesus didn't stumble into saving you. He did it purposefully. He did it perfectly. And He did it completely.

Prayer:

God, I thank you that you are in control. Thank you for sending your son to die, willingly, on that cross for me. God, thank you for a savior who oversaw His own life and death and saw fit that I should live through His sacrifice. Lord lead me to live in awe of Jesus Christ and in thanksgiving for the life his death grants to me.

Amen.

Now may the God who gives endurance and encouragement allow you to live in harmony with one another, according to the command of Christ Jesus, For I would not dare say anything except what Christ has accomplished through me to make the Gentiles obedient by word and deed, by the power of miraculous signs and wonders, and by the power of God's Spirit. As a result, I have fully proclaimed the good news about the Messiah from Jerusalem all the way around to Illyricum.

Romans 15:5,18-19 HSCB

What's your Jesus story? What is it that Christ has done in your life? Is it a story of radical change? Or one of hope in the midst of darkness? Maybe it's a story of lifelong faith and perseverance, or a story of change after a lifetime of running from Him. Whatever your story is, you need to tell it. People need to hear what Christ has done in your life, because people need to know that He died for them too. Someone out there has a similar story to your own minus one detail, Jesus. But that one detail is the one absolute thing that they may not even know they need, and you have the ability, and the duty, to let them know that. Your story has the ability to change lives. Your story has the potential to lead someone to the foot of the cross. It's the best tool we have, and the one spiritual gifts that is given to all believers. Practice telling your Jesus story. Get comfortable with telling others what Jesus has done in your life. And be excited about the story of how the savior revealed himself to you and came into your heart. It could save someone's life, for eternity.

Prayer:

Lord I want to thank you for my story. Thank you for touching my heart and for sending your son to die on the cross for me. Lord help me to be bold in telling my story. Use my story to impact those who have not come to know your son, and make my story all about you.

Amen.

6

For I am conscious of my rebellion, and my sin is always before me. Against You — You alone — I have sinned and done this evil in Your sight. So You are right when You pass sentence; You are blameless when You judge.

Psalms 51:3-4 HSCB

I'm not sure what David did more of...thank the Lord, or repent of the weakness of his flesh. One thing David always was, was conscious of his own shortcomings before the Lord. The life of David was spent in an attitude of repentance, and yours should be too. Don't get me wrong, to be in a constant state of repentance doesn't mean to be bogged down in your own sin and shame. That only brings you back to your sin like the dog returning to its vomit. Living in a constant state of repentance means you are always aware of how far you are from meeting the standards that God must set for His children, and this is great! We must live poor in spirit because, only when we understand the depth of our own depravity can we understand the greatness of the savior. When we make light of our flesh we make light of the sacrifice that Jesus Christ made. But when we are constantly aware that our flesh falls terribly short we are constantly aware of how great the sacrifice of Jesus Christ truly is. Fall on your face in thanksgiving today and don't forget to fall on your knees before God and repent. Only then will you see the greatness of our savior, and when you do you will exclaim "oh Lord how great thou art!"

Prayer:

Lord make me repentant. God burden my heart with the things that are in me which make you sad, and lead me ever into a spirit of repentance. Help me not to be bogged down in my sin and shame, but to be thankful that your son works to finish what He began in me when I first met Him.

Amen.

My lips will glorify You because Your faithful love is better than life. So I will praise You as long as I live; at Your name, I will lift up my hands.

Psalms 63:3-4 HCSB

If you had the chance to have the best life imaginable, anything you wanted when you wanted it, all the money you could dream, perfect relationships, never have to work a day, etc, but it was a life without God, would you take it? The answer should be a quick and resounding no. And yet we are so prone to walk away from the presence of our father for things far inferior to the life mentioned above. Why? Why would we choose that which is wasting away over the eternal? Why would we choose earthly pleasure over that which is far better than life? Are you doing that today? Have you walked away from the God who's love and kindness are greater than the bearing of your heart for things which will not last? Lift up your hands. Open up your lips to sing praises only to God today. Choose to cling to the One who is better than the best life you could ever imagine. Because a relationship with God truly is better than life. The salvation brought by the blood of Jesus is greater than the breath in your lungs. Thank God for His greatness today. Thank God for His love which is far better than anything we could attain in this life. A wonderful life without God ought to be the most terrible thing you could imagine. You could have everything, and if you didn't have Jesus it would be nothing. And you could have nothing, but if you have Jesus you have everything.

Prayer:

Lord show me your greatness today. Help me Lord to seek you and only you, and teach me daily that a life without you is no life at all. Lord instill in me the desire to seek after Jesus and remind me that I need Him each and every hour.

Amen.

A man who endures trials is blessed, because when he passes the test he will receive the crown of life that God has promised to those who love Him.

James 1:12 HCSB

Setbacks. Setbacks are a guarantee in this life. Sometimes they're our own fault, and sometimes they are struggles outside of our control, but you will have setbacks. But the setbacks don't determine who you are, what you do with them does. In this life you're guaranteed to get sick, you're at least going to catch a cold at some point. That kind of setback can be a pain. You miss work or church, or you don't go to the gym for a few days so you can get better. But you don't just quit after you do get better right? No, you go back to work ready to make up what you've missed. You jump back in the gym, energized, because you can't stand the feeling of getting nothing done. Most people don't let a setback like a nasty cold keep them down for very long. So why do we do that with sin? I've seen so many people fall into sin and decide that, since they already messed up they may as well stay there. Some stay for days, some for years, and some stay for a lifetime. But why? Why do we quit when we fall prey to our own flesh? When you get a cold you don't just say, "well this is who I am now". Right!? Because it's a sickness. You take medicine, you get better, and you get back to work. Treat sin the same way you would that nasty cold. Run to the one cure for the sickness of the flesh, Jesus. Let him beat it and then get up and move forward. James says the one who endures trials is blessed, not the one who stays in them. Whatever trial you're in today, self-made or out of your control, let Jesus be the cure. And then get up and get back to work. Your setbacks don't definitely you, but what you do with them will.

Prayer:

Lord help me to be ever moving forward in my pursuit of you. When I fall help me to get back up. When I fail, lead me to repent and begin my pursuit of you once again. Lord teach me that I am who I am, and who I am is your child.

Amen.

And just as it is appointed for people to die once — and after this, judgment — so also the Messiah, having been offered once to bear the sins of many, will appear a second time, not to bear sin, but to bring salvation to those who are waiting for Him.

Hebrews 9:27-28 HCSB

Judgement is coming, and so is Jesus. The lake of fire is as real as anything you see and feel in front of you, but so is the grace and mercy brought by the sacrifice of our Lord Jesus Christ. The wrath of God is powerful and will be wrought upon this world, but so will the salvation that Jesus Christ has offered freely to all who will believe and follow Him. We will all stand in front of the great white throne of judgement, but those who have been set apart by the blood of Jesus Christ will be pardoned completely grace. Many will perish, every moment of every day, for the rest of eternity, but those who turn their eyes upon Jesus, humble themselves, and ask for the forgiveness and mercy that He offers, will live abundantly for all of eternity. There is an everlasting difference between accepting Christ and rejecting Him. Which will you choose?

Prayer:

God I praise you for your justice. Thank you Lord for your judgement, and thank you for your mercy. Lord I thank you that, though I deserve your wrath, you chose to redeem me. God help me to turn towards your mercy each day as you lead me closer to you.

Amen

Just as you don't know the path of the wind, or how bones develop in the womb of a pregnant woman, so you don't know the work of God who makes everything.

Ecclesiastes 11:5 HCSB

Just because you can't see God working doesn't mean He is not. And just because you can't understand His plan doesn't mean He doesn't have one. I can look back over my life today and see that the Lord was moving every step of the way, but I couldn't always see when it was happening. But how could we ever expect to understand the creator of the universe? How could we expect our finite minds to wrap around all that the Lord is doing? To think that we must understand everything about God is nothing but arrogance, and to believe that the creation knows better than the creator is arrogance combined with ignorance. No, God is in total control, and the best thing we can do is hand it all over to Him. Go where the Holy spirit leads you to go. Do what the Lord places on your heart to do. And you will become what God created you to be. Any other path is the wrong one. Remember, the fool says in his heart "there is no God", but the fear of the Lord is the beginning of wisdom.

Prayer:

God thank you for your glorious plan for creation. Help me to trust in you completely, to go where you call me to go, and to do what you lay on my heart to do. Lord I pray that you would continue to lead me to walk in your way alone and let people see your son in me.

Amen

Why am I so depressed? Why is this turmoil within me? Put your hope in God, for I will still praise Him, my Savior and my God.

Psalms 42:11 HCSB

Is God really still God on your worst days? Of course He is! It's okay to feel depressed. It's okay to feel like nothing goes your way. It's okay to feel like the world has your number. But that never means that God has forsaken you. King David had one of the roughest beginnings throughout the Bible. He was promised the throne in Jerusalem years before he finally reached it, and the journey there was full of running for his life. He grew depressed. He grew tired. He grew anxious. But he never forgot the God who promised to put him on the throne in the first place. Pour your heart out to the Lord today. Let Him know how you're feeling! He wants to hear it, He wants you to say it out loud to Him, because He cares. But don't grow weary if things don't look up immediately. Notice the verse above. The psalmist didn't say anything about things getting better. He didn't say that God fixed his depression, or rid him of his turmoil. But he put his trust in the Lord anyways. He declared he would praise the Lord anyways. As Job said "yea though He slay me, still I will praise Him". Now that's faith. It's not fair weather faith. It's nitty gritty, down in the dirt, "I will always believe and trust" faith. That's the faith God desires of you. That's the faith that Jesus showed on the road to the cross. And that's the faith that will give you joy in the lowest of times.
Have faith.

Prayer:

Lord give me faith. Help me to see that you are always in control and that you do what is best for me. Lord, when I hurt, turn my eyes towards you and remind me that you are my God, and I am your child. Lead me in the way of everlasting and cause me to look to you in times of trouble.

Amen

> Do not be conquered by evil, but conquer evil with good.

Romans 12:21 HCSB

It's never enough to just give up a bad habit, it has to be replaced with a good one. When you go on a diet you don't just cut out the bad foods you have been eating, you replace them with good substantial foods to keep your muscles growing. If you don't you will lose muscle and get weaker. When you break away from poor form you don't just stop performing the lift. You replace your poor form with good form, if you don't you'll only get weaker. The same rule applies in your spiritual life. Think about your goals when it comes to temptation. What's the first thing that comes to mind? If you're like most people, you'll probably say "I just want to stop sinning". Man, I can't tell you how many times I have said the same thing! But here's the truth...that never works! Unless you replace your sinful habits with godly habits your spirit will only get weaker. Jesus described it as the man who kicked out the demon living in his house. When the demon was tired of roaming around he came back, found the house clean and swept, and brought seven more demons to trash the place again. That's what happens when we try to just "stop sinning". Try this instead. Make your goal to become more desperate for Jesus than you were yesterday. Replace your own sinful flesh with the heart of Christ! It's the only way to succeed in ridding yourself of the habitual sins that eat you alive. Don't just combat evil, weaponless, hopeless, and defeated. Combat evil with good. Combat evil with Jesus, and you will be victorious

Prayer:

God I pray that my goals would align with your will. As I push to walk closer with you I pray that the wickedness of my flesh would be replaced with the righteousness of Jesus. As I walk, replace me with you. Lead me Lord.

Amen

But thanks be to God, who gives us the victory through our Lord Jesus Christ! Therefore, my dear brothers, be steadfast, immovable, always excelling in the Lord's work, knowing that your labor in the Lord is not in vain.

1 Corinthians 15:57-58 HCSB

Consistency is the key to growth. Ask any successful bodybuilder, CEO, preacher, or anyone else who has tasted success and they will tell you that the one thing that lead them to their success was consistency. We live in a culture that is so focused on the now that we are repulsed by things that take time and effort to achieve. But nothing comes over night. There is magic pill to make you fit without years of hard work and dedication. Finding the perfect job almost never happens in the first interview. It takes years if climbing the ladder, working with integrity, and proving your worth to make those dreams happen. And it is the same for your spiritual life. Understanding scripture doesn't happen overnight. Developing a healthy prayer life doesn't come without work and perseverance. Making a habit of godly decision making only comes from making godly decisions over and over again. The Christian walk is certainly not for those who are looking for a quick fix. The only thing that Jesus offers freely is grace, but a life worthy of the calling of Jesus Christ will cost you all of you, over and over again, until your life ends. But let me tell you, it's worth it! Never has a Christian looked back on a lifetime of furthering the kingdom and regretted it. Never has a follower of Jesus Christ reached the end if their life and said, "I wish I hadn't done that". A life walked with God is rewarding, but it is also trying. To succeed requires consistency, and the work never ends. But the reward is eternally wonderful.

Prayer:

God make me consistent. Bring me back to Jesus over and over until He is my first destination. Lord help me to continue to choose you each and every day, and lead me ever closer to you.

Amen

For God's wrath is revealed from heaven against all godlessness and unrighteousness of people who by their unrighteousness suppress the truth, since what can be known about God is evident among them, because God has shown it to them.

Romans 1:18-19 HCSB

We must never forget the wrath of God. It is so easy for us to focus on the live and mercy of God, which is real and is all powerful. But we often neglect the wrath of God that is promised to all unrighteousness and godlessness, because it's a sore subject. Often times we think that, if we down play the wrath of God it makes Him look more appealing to those who don't know Him. After all, who wants to come to a God who would send somebody to hell, right? But this is dangerous. Without the wrath of God, the mercy and love that is offered by God is not needed.

God has saved us for Himself, by Himself. But why did we need salvation in the first place? Because He needed to save us from Himself. Don't render your evangelism useless by skipping over the terror of the wrath of God that is to come, it does the hearer a great disservice. People who are sick must know they are sick in order to seek the cure, and those who face the wrath of God must know that it is coming before they can seek the grace and mercy that is offered. It is arrogant to think that we must "clean God up" to make Him appealing to the lost.

Prayer:

God let me not forget your wrath. Remind me of all that I have been saved from, and lead me to preach your truth to those around me who don't know your son. Lord thank you for the greatness of your mercy and lead me to be thankful each day for your justice and mercy.

Amen

Therefore I, the prisoner for the Lord, urge you to walk worthy of the calling you have received, with all humility and gentleness, with patience, accepting one another in love, diligently keeping the unity of the Spirit with the peace that binds us.

Ephesians 4:1-3 HCSB

Are you for the Lord? Paul wrote to Ephesus from a Roman prison. Though he was a prisoner of the Romans, he chose to be a prisoner FOR the Lord. And notice how much that meant to Him. It was his whole identity at this moment in his life. Everything Paul was, it was for the Lord. When Paul went to prison there were many who thought his ministry was over, but some of his most compelling books were written while in prison, because Paul was for the Lord. Where are you at right now? Are you desperate? Be desperate for the Lord! Are you a worker, CEO, job hunting? Dedicate whatever you are doing to the Lord! Reach out to someone who needs Jesus today, and use the situation that you are in to lead others to the foot of the cross. Paul was in the most dire of situations. He had no idea whether he would live or die. Roman prisons were far from a good time. And yet Paul gave his situation over to Jesus, and became a prisoner for the Lord. So what are you going to do with what you are? Decide today to be a husband for the Lord. Be a father for the Lord. Be a coworker for the Lord. Be a man or woman for the Lord. Whatever you do, do it as unto the Lord.

Prayer:

God make me to be after your heart. Lead me to be a slave in your name, and to be who I am in and through you. God I thank you that you are working diligently in me, help me to work diligently in your name, through your power.

Amen

But seek first the kingdom of God and His righteousness, and all these things will be provided for you. Therefore don't worry about tomorrow, because tomorrow will worry about itself. Each day has enough trouble of its own.

Matthew 6:33-34 HCSB

What are you seeking first? What was the first thing on your mind when you got out of bed this morning? Is it money? Your job? Another job? A better life, car, house, physique? What is it that takes up the most real estate in your mind? Because that is your god. All of the things of this world are passing away. Even the nicest car breaks down and dies. One day you will retire from that dream job. You're going to get old and lose that physique. Nothing in this world is eternal. But the kingdom of God is. Eternity is hard to imagine. We can not wrap our minds around something that really has no end and no beginning, but the Kingdom of God is eternal. So why wouldn't you seek His kingdom first? This life that you live is smaller than a dot on the timeline when compared to the life that is to come. So why do we spend so much time worrying about the now? Instead, be desperate for Jesus Christ. Hit your knees in desperate need of Him today. Tomorrow is going to come, and it will bring troubles. There is nothing you can do to stop it, but you can lean on the King who already knows and has already been there. Because He does care for you. Seek the kingdom first. Evangelize the lost. Dive into the Word that was there in the beginning. Talk to Jesus. Before your feet hit the ground, be after the kingdom, and everything else will take care of itself.

Prayer:

God lead me to seek your kingdom first each day. Before my feet hit the ground make yourself known to me. Before I close my eyes to sleep remind me that I am yours, and you are mine. Remind me each day that you are all that matters.

Amen

Unless the Lord builds a house, its builders labor over it in vain; unless the Lord watches over a city, the watchman stays alert in vain.

Psalms 127:1 HCSB

What are you trying to do apart from the Lord right now? Are you trying to make your career work out? Finances? Your marriage? All of these things are important for you to work on, but apart from the Lord you will fail. Every decision, every work, everything we do must be weighed against scripture and prayed over. As King Solomon so wisely said "trust in the Lord with all your heart, lean not on your own understanding", because your own understanding is finite. It's limited. But the understanding of the Lord is eternal. He has already walked through every moment of your life. He's been there, He knows what is going to happen. So how dumb must it look when we try to take things into our own small hands? So think about it. What do you need to pray over today? What have you been working on that just doesn't seem to want to work out, no matter how hard you try? Try giving it over to the Lord, He promises to work it out according to His will. Things may not go the way you planned if you hand them over to God, but I promise you that it's better that way. Thank the Lord most of my life didn't go the way I planned it.

Prayer:

God help me to allow my plans to align with your plans. Give me the strength to hand my life over to you, all of it, and allow you to do with me what you will. Remind me that this life is not my own, that I was bought for a price, and that all I do belongs to you.

Amen

Dear friends, we are God's children now, and what we will be has not yet
been revealed. We know that when He appears, we will be like Him
because we will see Him as He is.

1 John 3:2 HCSB

I thank the Lord every day that He isn't finished with me yet, because I
am still broken. And so are you. There is no one who does not need long
and intense work from Jesus Christ. Day in and day out the Holy spirit is
chiseling out the masterpiece that He made you out to be. But it's a tough
and painful process. When the Lord shows you that He needs to chisel
away that pride, don't shy away from the pain that comes with it,
embrace it. Embrace the fact that you're going to come face to face with
the darkest and ugliest parts of who you are, because that is what it takes
for you to begin handing over those parts to be chiseled out by Jesus
Christ. It's hard to look in the mirror and see weakness, pride, lust,
addiction, gluttony, and sinfulness in general. When Isaiah was faced
with what he saw in his own heart he was devastated. But the thing that
you must remember when you see you is this, Jesus is working! He's
breaking away those things in you that make you cringe to your core.
And He isn't done yet. Identify those things that you need to hand over to
Jesus today. Are you failing your spouse? Hand it to Jesus and let Him
rip out that failure to be replaced with His love and passion. Can't get
away from this vile pornographic culture that we live in? Run from your
lust into the arms of Jesus and allow Him to chisel that lust out of your
life. It won't be easy. You will have failures. But Jesus isn't done with
you, and He won't be until you look like His spitting image. Mourn over
your brokenness today, and then turn to the One who can make you
brand new. Because He will, and He is working on you right now.

Prayer:

Lord please keep making me. I love you God, but I fail daily. Lord keep
chiseling out your son's image in my life. I thank you that you don't give
up on me, that you're faithful even when I am faithless. Lord please keep
making me.

Amen

Who may ascend the mountain of the Lord ? Who may stand in His holy place? The one who has clean hands and a pure heart, who has not set his mind on what is false, and who has not sworn deceitfully.

Psalms 24:3-4 HCSB

Purity. It's not just about doing good deeds. It's not about helping your neighbor, or not cussing when you stub your toe. It's so much deeper than that. Sure, good deeds are important. Living a life that exemplifies goodness is absolutely vital in the ministry that all Christians have been called to. But purity is so much deeper. Purity is having a clean heart, clean hands, godly intention, and an intentional spirit. Your good deeds can not create a clean heart within you. Your own righteous acts can not sweep out the filth that takes root in your heart. Purity comes from the heart of Jesus Christ and changes our hearts. Purity doesn't say, "here are my good works for your use God". Purity says, "here is my heart, use it to do your will". Purity understands that, because of the human condition of sin, we have nothing to bring to the table, but because of the sacrifice of Jesus Christ we bring all of ourselves to the table to be molded and used by God. When you focus too much on what you do and don't do, it becomes your religion. Your worship is wasted on how good you are. Instead, hand your heart over to the Savior. Allow Him to make it pure. Let your good works stem from His heart and will. Don't neglect doing what is good, but do not worship it either. Because so much more good will be done, through you, by Jesus than will be done by you, for Jesus. Focus on purity today. Ask the Lord to create in you a clean heart. And then, by His power, go forth and do good.

Prayer:

Create in me a clean heart Lord. Lead me not only to do good, but to be made good each day by your holy spirit. Turn my eyes to you Lord and purify me until the day that you return for me. Lead me in purity and cause me to be made into the image of Jesus.

Amen

Thomas responded to Him, "My Lord and my God! " Jesus said, "Because you have seen Me, you have believed. Those who believe without seeing are blessed."

John 20:28-29 HCSB

How often we ask for signs and wonders, and that really is okay. It's alright to ask of God, "are you really there?" But do not let yourself fall into the trap of only trusting God when the signs and wonders abound. The key evidence of faith is when we believe even in the midst of the nastiest storm. Those who only believe in the Lord when He performs signs, or shows them wonders, never really believed at all. You may be in the fight of your life right now, but don't lose faith! The Savior said that if you believe in Him even when you can not see you will be blessed. You will be blessed with peace in the midst of strife. You will be blessed with love in the most hateful of times. You will be blessed with the tender love and mercy of the Lord Jesus Christ every single day. But when Jesus went back to His hometown, and they did not believe in Him, He could do no miracles because of their unbelief. Instead He had to shake the dust off His feet and walk away. Don't let your heart be tossed to and fro like the waves. Don't let your belief in the Lord Jesus Christ waver because of your circumstances. Instead, allow the Lord to bless you with His peace and mercy day in and day out. All you must do is trust Him with all your heart, lean not on your own understanding, and acknowledge Him even when He seems to be hidden from your eyes, because He is there and He is holding you in His nail scarred hands.

Prayer:

God give me faith. Lead me to see you even when it seems that you are silent. I know that you are at work even when I can't see you, God help me to believe when belief seems impossible.

Amen

No one is ferocious enough to rouse Leviathan; who then can stand against Me? Who confronted Me, that I should repay him? Everything under heaven belongs to Me.

Job 41:10-11 HCSB

Did you know there were dragons in the Bible? Take a look at the Leviathan. His breath is fire, his scales are impenetrable. People faint at the very sight of him. Some versions of the Bible try to call this a crocodile, but I don't think so. And guess what? God is in total control of the Leviathan. In fact, there is nothing under the heavens that does not belong to God, including you. He doesn't owe you or me anything. No prayer you bring before Him deserves to be answered, no question you ask Him deserves a response. And yet He has mercy on you and me. That's right. He restored Job after he questioned Him. And He restores you and me even when we crucify His son. That's the grace of the Almighty God. So what are you holding on to? And why are you still holding on to it? Are you trying to battle your own sinfulness by yourself? That's a Leviathan of its own, stop it. Hand the control over to God. Let Jesus destroy the power of sin over your life. Are you trying to control your own joy? Or are you trying to control the people in your life? Stop it. Hand it all over to the Lord. He's more than qualified to hold you in His arms. He's beyond capable of leading you in the right direction. Stop trying to force that job, or make that relationship happen. Stop using sin to ease your anxiety or fill the void in your heart. The one who controls the Leviathan loves you and wants control, not to bend you to His will, but to lead you in it. Stop trying to take what belongs to God. Let go of the reigns and place them in His hands today.

Prayer:

Lord I want to stop to praise you. I praise you for your strength. I praise you for your awesome power. And I praise you for your tender love towards me. Lead me to hand over the control in my life to you, because you are far more qualified to lead this life than I am.

Amen

The Lord does not delay His promise, as some understand delay, but is patient with you, not wanting any to perish but all to come to repentance.

2 Peter 3:9 HCSB

Do you sometimes feel like the Lord has forgotten about us? I mean it's been 2,000 years. The world is plenty messed up enough for Him to come back. So why isn't He here yet? Peter tells us the Lord hasn't forgotten His promise, He will return. But the second coming of Jesus Christ is no small ordeal. For the Christian the coming of Christ will be glorious. It will be time for us to go home, to meet our groom and be taken up to live in the presence of God for all of eternity. It will be the wedding feast to end all feasts. But think about what the return of Jesus means for the lost. The worst of fates would be a cakewalk compared to being lost at the return of Jesus. Even just the things that will happen here on Earth will be beyond anything a horror movie could portray. John says that people will flee to the mountains and beg to be crushed by rocks so that the suffering under the total wrath of God will end. But our God is long-suffering. He won't force anyone, but He wills that all would come to the saving knowledge of His son. So don't be discouraged that the Lord tarries His return, it's because He loves and longs to forgive as many as possible. Don't let the world tell you that He is not coming because He waits, instead tell them He waits for them. Seek out the lost. Because one day He will return like a thief in the night, and every knee will bow and every tongue will confess. But for those who have rejected Him up till then, it will be too late.

Prayer:

God break my heart for the lost. Thank you for your longsuffering and the mercy that is new every day. God lead me to those who need your son, and give me the boldness to lead as many as possible to the foot of the cross.

Amen

They asked this to trap Him, in order that they might have evidence to accuse Him. Jesus stooped down and started writing on the ground with His finger. When they persisted in questioning Him, He stood up and said to them, "The one without sin among you should be the first to throw a stone at her." Then He stooped down again and continued writing on the ground.

John 8:6-8 HCSB

The story of the adulterous woman who Jesus saved. It's one of the most quoted stories in the Bible today. "you who is without sin, cast the first stone". We marvel over what Jesus said here. But I want to know what He wrote in the ground. See, the Pharisees and Sadducees saw themselves as being without sin. They felt that they were chosen by God to judge the common people. So why would they walk away when Jesus said this? I think it's because of whatever he wrote in the dirt. Was it each of their hidden sins? Or maybe their thoughts at that moment? Whatever it was, it was powerful, because Jesus is powerful. He has the power to convict even the hardest of hearts. He has the power to forgive even the worst of sins. And He has the power to tell you and me, "go and sin no more". There is nothing in this world that can not be held in the hand of Jesus. There is no one in this world who does not desperately need Him. At this moment in this passage, the Pharisees and Sadducees had a few options. They chose to walk away from the one who holds salvation. No, they didn't stone this woman, but they also hardened their hearts to Jesus Christ. When you are convicted by the Lord, when the spirit shows you that you heart is hardened, don't walk away. Don't choose to keep the sin that so easily ensnares you. Be like the woman in this passage who, when she saw her depravity, did not harden her heart, but surrendered herself to Jesus Christ. I believe Jesus convicted both the religious leaders, and the adulterous woman in this passage. One group chose to walk away, angry, and one woman chose to look into the eyes of the savior and see her need. I think we will find out what Jesus wrote in the sand when we get to heaven, but don't wait till then. Turn to Him today.

Prayer:

Lord reveal to me where I fall short and cause me to see my need for you. I pray that my heart will not be hardened. Change me Lord. Amen

24

Then He proceeded to denounce the towns where most of His miracles were done, because they did not repent: "Woe to you, Chorazin! Woe to you, Bethsaida! For if the miracles that were done in you had been done in Tyre and Sidon, they would have repented in sackcloth and ashes long ago! But I tell you, it will be more tolerable for Tyre and Sidon on the day of judgment than for you. And you, Capernaum, will you be exalted to heaven? You will go down to Hades. For if the miracles that were done in you had been done in Sodom, it would have remained until today. But I tell you, it will be more tolerable for the land of Sodom on the day of judgment than for you."

Matthew 11:20-24 HCSB

There is a message in this passage of scripture that is so important to our time today. Repent! Turn to Jesus Christ! Or be destroyed. It's so sad to look around and see miracles being worked, lives being touched directly by Jesus Christ, and still people walking the road to destruction. It's not enough just to acknowledge that God exists. It's not enough to know that Jesus was a miracle worker, or an important person. It's not even enough to know that Jesus was divine in some way. The only thing that will matter on judgement day is this, did you accept Jesus Christ as the Lord and savior of your life? Jesus says here that those who knew Him, tasted of His grace, saw His divinity and the miracles wrought in their lives, and still refuse Him will be worse off on judgement day than even Sodom and Gammorah. Don't miss out on the greatest gift ever given to mankind. Don't be like those in Roman's 1 who, though they knew God, refused to give Him glory for sending His son for the salvation of this world. You could live a thousand lives, be the best person this world has seen, accomplish more than all of the saints combined, but if you do all that and never accept Christ as the Lord and savior of your life it is all for nought. Jesus Christ isn't just everything, He is the only thing. Repent or be destroyed isn't just a catchy slogan that Christians use, it is the reality of this broken world, and our tainted hearts.

Prayer:

Lord don't let the weight of your sacrifice pass me by. Continue to show me just how wonderful the gift of your grace is, and remind me that you are the only thing. Amen

The one who will not use the rod hates his son, but the one who loves him disciplines him diligently.

Proverbs 13:24 HCSB

"We make men without chests and expect from them virtue and enterprise. We laugh at honour and are shocked to find traitors in our midst"

- C.S. Lewis

What is it that turns a young boy into a good man? Discipline. Discipline is vital in the development of manliness. But our society has cried for so long that masculinity is backwards, that it's outdated, that we have stopped trying to produce men, and so we have lost the art of discipline. The truth is there is no such thing as toxic masculinity, only the lack of masculinity. Good discipline sticks with a man throughout his whole life and, more importantly, turns into self discipline. Without self discipline the man ceases to be a man. Masculinity can not develop in an environment with no discipline. A young man will not grow in an environment where he is told that consequences don't exist. Our culture wants men to be able to terminate any mistake they make, to simply abort the consequences of any poor decision they make. And this is why the majority of men are no longer men. Don't let this world lie to you. Don't avoid discipline, except by doing the right thing. Because lack of discipline breeds soft men, and it is soft men who commit evil. Instead, welcome the consequences of every action. Thank God that He sees fit to discipline and train His children. And let an attitude of self discipline grow inside your heart. And pass it on to your son's. It's the only way for a boy to become a man.

Prayer:

God help me to love discipline. Not to seek it, but to embrace it when I need it. Lord lead me to learn from discipline and to learn self-discipline as I grow closer to you each day.

Amen

The depths of the sea became visible, the foundations of the world were exposed, at Your rebuke, Lord , at the blast of the breath of Your nostrils.

Psalms 18:15 HCSB

What a mighty God we serve! If He were to descend from the heavens the world would not be able to hold His majesty! The seas would split and the Earth would open up. We would all be destroyed from the sheer magnificence of His holiness. His rebuke is final, His power is unmatched, and yet His grace is never ending. Praise the Lord because He is worthy to be praised. When was the last time you stopped and simply worshipped God? Not at church or a worship service. Not because He answered a prayer or gave you a good word. But simply because He is God. I mean no amount of praise we could give Him would ever measure up to the praise that He deserves, and yet I fail to stop and acknowledge that He is the almighty all the time. I get too busy for the God who created the universe? How crazy is that? Take time out of your day today to simply praise God because He is the great I AM. "Lord your power is great, your holiness is pure, and yet your grace to me is unending". Sometimes that's all we need to pray. We don't need a special reason, or a special occasion to lift His name on high. Shout out a praise to the Lord today, he is deserving of all that you can give, and more.

Prayer:

Lord I lift your name on high. I want to take a moment to praise you, not for anything I have received, but because you are worthy of all my praise. God remind me of your majesty and lead me to see how Holy you truly are.

Amen

Now this is the message we have heard from Him and declare to you: God is light, and there is absolutely no darkness in Him. If we say, "We have fellowship with Him," yet we walk in darkness, we are lying and are not practicing the truth.

1 John 1:5-6 HCSB

Why would a loving God send anyone to hell? It's a tough question to answer, because we don't really want to say what needs to be said about it. The fact is that God is loving, but He is also just. God grants mercy and Grace, but He also pours out wrath and justice. He must. A God who is not just could never be loving, and a God who is holy can not dwell among sin. In our finite minds it may seem unloving to send anyone to eternal torture, but the reality is that eternal torture is exactly what you and I deserve. There is no light in us apart from Jesus. I can do good deeds, feel empathy, and have compassion on others, but I can never be good enough to stand in the presence of God because my heart was born into darkness. But God, in His infinite mercy, offers a way for you and I to be fully justified to stand in His presence. If you don't accept that gift it's not on Him. He has already offered far more than you or I could ever imagine. He sent His own son to die for those who hated Him. He had to turn His back on His own child, for the first time in all of eternity, because He could not look on the sin that was heaped upon the shoulders of Jesus Christ for you. To say that God is not loving because He sends people to hell who refuse to choose life is no more than a half hearted excuse to deny His existence. But we must be ready to answer this question, and to fully trust that God has been infinitely more loving than He ever needed to be by offering Jesus as your replacement on the cross.

Prayer:

God thank you for your mercy. Remind me of just how lost I am without you, and lead me to always come back to the cross. Thank you Lord for your mercy and the depth of your love.

Amen

28

As obedient children, do not be conformed to the desires of your former ignorance. But as the One who called you is holy, you also are to be holy in all your conduct; for it is written, Be holy, because I am holy.

1 Peter 1:14-16 HCSB

Don't be ignorant. It really is that simple. When we turn from the greatness of Jesus Christ, and forsake His wonderful grace and mercy to turn to sin, we return to the ignorance that Christ died to pull us out of. It sounds harsh, nobody likes being called ignorant because it hurts. But we have to look at our own sin this way. Your sin must become so disgusting to you that the very thought of departing from the Lord's will makes you sick. Because sin truly is that disgusting. Instead let the holiness of God reign in your heart. As you begin to see sin for the gross ignorance that it is, look to the Lord and allow Him to show your heart how wonderful His holiness is, and strive for it! You won't get it perfect in this life. You will fail, you will fall back into your former ignorance at times. But when you begin to see the ways of this world for what they are, and see God for who He is, His holiness begins to reign in you. We, as Christians, must stop treating sin as something we merely ought to avoid, but as something that surely leads to awful and painful death. You wouldn't stick your feet anywhere near the mouth of a wood chipper right? But that is exactly what we are doing when we treat the sin in this world nonchalantly. Treat it like a wood chipper, stay far away from it as often as humanly possible, and strive towards the holiness of God daily.

Prayer:

God cause me to hate my sin and the sin around me. Lord I pray that I would see the flesh as you see it, violent and dangerous. Lead me far from my sin and into your arms each day.

Amen

"I am the bread of life," Jesus told them. "No one who comes to Me will ever be hungry, and no one who believes in Me will ever be thirsty again.

John 6:35 HCSB

What are you filling up on?

Jesus is the bread of life. Accept Him into your heart and make Him Lord over your life, and you will never need anything else. Sure, you're going to need food and water to keep your body alive, but spiritually you will be filled for eternity, never to hunger again. But the reverse of what Jesus said is this, nothing but Him will ever fill you permanently. A relationship, even a great one, will never make you whole. Drugs, alcohol, pornography, all of these things may quench your thirst or sedate your anxiety for a little bit, but they always leave you needing more and more. But Jesus! Jesus will make you want more of Him because only He can satisfy for good. Only Jesus can bring you peace that passes all understanding. Nothing apart from Jesus can satisfy what you need or desire. If you were to give everything you owned away to the poor, but missed out on Jesus, it would all be in vain. If you got married and raised the most beautiful family that has ever lived, but missed out on Jesus, it would be meaningless. Stop trying to fill your void with temporary things. Nothing will ever work until you surrender to Jesus Christ and partake of the bread of life that will make your life runneth over and spill out for all the world to see Him. If you had nothing but Jesus you would have everything, and if you had everything but Jesus you would have nothing. Don't seek to gain the world and neglect your soul. Don't invest in what will not last. Let Jesus Christ fill you to the brim and you will never be empty again.

Prayer:

God remind me of how wonderful your son is. Help me not to fill up my life with this world, but to be filled to the brim with Jesus.

Amen

Then Peter came to Him and said, "Lord, how many times could my brother sin against me and I forgive him? As many as seven times? " "I tell you, not as many as seven," Jesus said to him, "but 70 times seven.

Matthew 18:21-22 HCSB

Aren't we all just like Peter? Coming to Jesus, trying to figure out the bare minimum we can do while still being a Christian? I do it, you do it, we all do it. But here is what Peter failed to understand in this passage, and what I often fail to understand in my own life, we are unlovable. The way that we have turned our backs on God is unforgivable. But God demonstrated His own love towards us in this, that while we were unlovable He loved us. While we were unforgivable He forgave us. That's what grace is, it's showing love to those who don't deserve it. Mercy is forgiving those who have hurt you the most, even before they apologize. We have to understand this truth, that you can only love Jesus Christ as much as you love the person you love least. Forgiveness isn't just a suggestion, it is mandatory in the life of the Christian. In the few verses after this passage Jesus goes into what I like to call a "Peter induced parable". Read it. You have been forgiven of so much, forgiveness offered long before you ever asked for it. But if you are unwilling to extend that forgiveness to others then why should it be offered to you any longer? Extend love to the unlovable in your life. Forgive the unforgivable. Don't wait for them to ask, just do it. And if you have offended a brother, seek restoration today. Christ loved the unlovable in you and has forgiven far more than 70 times seven of your own sins. Don't let forgiveness end with you, extend it to any and all, it's what God intended.

Prayer:

Lord I have sinned against you so many times and yet you continue to offer forgiveness. Lord forgive me where I need forgiveness, and lead me to forgive those who have wronged me. If I need to seek forgiveness from anyone humble me enough to do so.

Amen

The Father loves the Son and has given all things into His hands. The one who believes in the Son has eternal life, but the one who refuses to believe in the Son will not see life; instead, the wrath of God remains on him.

John 3:35-36 HCSB

There is so much crazy stuff that goes on in the world today that it's easy, if we listen to the wrong voices, to act like Jesus has lost a little bit of control of the world. But make no mistake, everything is in His hands. Unless you place your total trust in Jesus Christ as your Lord and savior there is no life. It's easy to let yourself slip into the habit of taking your life in your own hands. You make plans apart from the wisdom of the word, try to stand toe to toe with temptation, return evil for evil, and take retribution into your own hands. The reason we often do this is because we let ourselves feel like Jesus isn't totally in control of some situations. That person who hurt you needs to get what's coming to them? But Jesus just doesn't seem to be doing it the way you would like Him to. Or that job opportunity is absolutely perfect, But Jesus just isn't opening the door the way you expected. Don't try to get ahead of the Lord! That doesn't mean don't work for anything, but if a door isn't opening, or if someone who hurt you seems to be getting along just fine, trust that Jesus Christ has the best for you in the works. Because He does and, to be honest, He is far more qualified to guide your life than you are.

Prayer:

Lord remind me that you are in control. Show me that my life is not my own and that you are at work in and around me. Lord give me the strength to step out of your way and grow in you.

Amen

Jesus Christ is the same yesterday, today, and forever. Don't be led astray by various kinds of strange teachings; for it is good for the heart to be established by grace and not by foods, since those involved in them have not benefited.

Hebrews 13:8-9 HCSB

Jesus Christ has never changed. Never. Since before time began Christ was the same as He is today, and will be for the rest of eternity. That means there was never a plan b. God always knew that we would fail Him. There has never been a point in all of eternity that Jesus Christ wasn't sure whether He would need to die for you or not. And yet He created you anyways. He took the time and the skillful effort to knit together your inner most being in the womb. He took care to create in you a heart that longed for Him so that, when He set you free, you would be able to know peace. Jesus never changes. The gospel never changes, it has been the same since the day it was written. God, in His tender love, created us and we failed Him. And in His never-ending mercy God created for us a way to be restored into a relationship with Him, through Jesus, the propitiation for our shortcomings. That was always the plan. The gospel was written out long before any author was divinely inspired to put it on paper. Things of this world will change. People change. Culture changes. Human love will change. The methods we use for spreading the gospel will change. But Jesus Christ will remain the same throughout all of eternity, and the word of the Lord endures forever. Don't let the world fool you, it's not here for good. Place all of your trust in the unending, unchanging, savior of the world, Jesus Christ.

Prayer:

God thank you for Jesus and for your unchanging love. Help me to be grounded in your word and to be unwavering in my faith in you. Lead me to follow you each day and not to waver when this world tries to pull me from you.

Amen

This Jesus is the stone rejected by you builders, which has become the cornerstone. There is salvation in no one else, for there is no other name under heaven given to people, and we must be saved by it."

Acts 4:11-12 HCSB

"In Christ alone" isn't just a catchy song. It's absolute truth. There is nothing that can save you except for Jesus Christ. There is no way to attain peace, love, joy, success, but through Jesus Christ. No president, administration, economic model, or law can give you abundant Life. Only Jesus Christ can do that. No amount of exercise or hard work can give you strength or success in this life. Only Jesus Christ can to that.

Unless we surrender our lives to the Lordship of Jesus Christ we are hopelessly lost in our own flesh. Unless we unify under Jesus Christ as Lord, there will never be true unity in our churches, our homes, or our country. Unless we surrender our nation to the Lordship of Jesus Christ we will fail to stand as a nation. And there is no truth except for in Jesus Christ. The devil works hardest to convince us that there are other ways, other things we can lean on. If Satan can convince you that Jesus is one of many ways to accomplish freedom then he has already defeated you.

We must not allow ourselves to be deceived, the only way to life is through Jesus Christ. To think that we have made it without Jesus is to lose everything. But to lose everything and still have Jesus would be to gain eternity. Anything that does not have Jesus as the cornerstone will crumble. But a life built upon Him will stand for eternity, glorified forever by God.

Prayer:

Jesus be the cornerstone of my life. God help me not to worship you in song alone but in my words, actions, and my ways. Lead me ever into a deeper relationship with you and help me to seek Christ alone.

Amen

I will give thanks to You because You have answered me and have become my salvation. The stone that the builders rejected has become the cornerstone. This came from the Lord ; it is wonderful in our eyes. This is the day the Lord has made; let us rejoice and be glad in it.

Psalms 118:21-24 HCSB

This is the day that the Lord has made! What are you going to do with it? Today may be a rough day, or it might be a great day. Things could go absolutely swimmingly today, or they could take a turn for the worst. But the Lord woke you up today. Will you praise His name with what you do with the day He has given you? Will you do everything today as if you are doing it unto the Lord? Will you step out and walk far around temptation? Or will today be dedicated to Satan? See because any day the Lord gives us that we fail to dedicate back to Him is a win for the devil in our lives. God woke me up today! God created the day that I am setting out on! How could we not give it back to Him? How could we not rejoice and be glad that today is His day, and we get to take part in it? I urge you to use today to lift up the name of Jesus Christ. Tell somebody what He has done for you. Work like the Lord has provided you with air to breathe and energy to get things done. Don't let today belong to the devil in your life, give it back to God and lift this name high with what you do with His day.

Prayer:

Lord cause me to dedicate this day to you. Lead me to live in the day that you have given me in a way that glorifies you. Don't allow the enemy to rule this day, I pray that this day would be your day in my life.

Amen

Our God is in heaven and does whatever He pleases.

Psalms 115:3 HCSB

"God is in control". We say it so often. When we go through hard times, when we're anxious, lose loved ones. But when times get easy we tend to completely forget this fact. When life is easy it is so simple to think that I've got it on my own. But I don't. When things are tough God is in control. When life seems to be going right God is in control. When I face temptation, God is in control. So why do we try so hard to do it on our own? When you face temptation on your own power, you will lose. No matter how much I want to do what's right, no matter how hard I try, every time I try to fight the devil on my own I lose. "Let go and let God" isn't just a catchy slogan, it must be a way of life. When you find yourself facing sin, run into the arms of Jesus Christ. When you hurt, run into the arms of Jesus Christ. And when everything is going great, still run into the arms of Jesus Christ. "I need thee, oh I need thee, every hour I need thee" is a wonderful hymn. Don't treat Jesus like a genie in a bottle. In the good times and the bad praise Him because He is in control. And let go, and let God always.

Prayer:

Lord I need you, oh I need you, every hour I need you. Let this be my prayer Lord each and every day. Lead me to want you every hour, to seek your face, and to walk in your ways each day.

Amen

Then Saul said to David, Blessed be thou, my son David: thou shalt both do great things, and also shalt still prevail. So David went on his way, and Saul returned to his place.

1 Samuel 26:25 KJV

Be careful not to harden your heart to God. Saul was so caught up in his own sin that he completely hardened his heart before the Lord. It's clear that, even in the state that Saul's heart was in, the Lord was still working on it. When Saul realised that David had spared his life he has a moment of softness in his heart and even admitted that God had ordained David to be king. And then in the next verse Saul is hunting David down once again. This hard heartedness didn't happen over night. Saul allowed himself to get so used to living in disobedience to sin that, over time, he snuffed out the still small voice of the Holy spirit in his heart. I fully believe that if Saul had humbled himself before the Lord, God would have restored Saul's heart unto Him. Not that the Lord would have given Saul his throne back, but he could have received the peace and grace of God again. We can't allow ourselves dive so far into our disobedience to God that we snuff out the voice of the Holy Spirit in our lives. The Lord will wait for you with open arms, but He won't drag you back to Him kicking and screaming. Don't allow your heart to be hardened towards the Lord, if you feel far from Him turn back today, soften your heart, and open your ears to His still small voice.

Prayer:

Lord if there is any hardness in my heart I pray that you would reveal it and remove it. Lead me into obedience each day and make my heart tender towards you Lord.

Amen

Flee also youthful lusts; but pursue righteousness, faith, love, peace with those who call on the Lord out of a pure heart.

II Timothy 2:22 NKJV

In his second letter to the young pastor, Paul warns Timothy to turn tail and run from youthful lusts. Flee is the word he uses. That means to turn around and run for your life from sin. Why? Because sin distorts your mind. Youthful lusts, drunkenness, gossip, pornography, all of these things dig their claws deep into your mind and refuse to let go. Youthful lusts turn into adult lusts, which turn into addictions to sinful behavior. Some people find that they simply can't stop gossiping, or lying. Some grow up and realize that they can't shake that disgusting porn habit. Some grow to middle age only to realize that alcohol won't let them go. Sin doesn't leave us when we reach a certain age. It leads us farther and farther away from Jesus Christ until, (Satan hopes), we can no longer hear that still small voice that convicts our hearts. Don't be deceived, sin doesn't play nice. It will clean itself up and seem fun for a while, but it leaves you so empty afterwards that you find yourself having to fill up more and more often. But Jesus never leaves you empty. If you turn your eyes from the flesh that fights to destroy you and run full speed into the arms of Jesus He will fill you until your cup runs over and you will never need another hit of that nasty drug called sin that has held you down and beat you up for so long. He will redeem you.

Prayer:

God give me the desires of your heart. Lead me to flee from the sin that wants to lead me away from you. Lord help me to hate what is evil in your sight and run each day towards Jesus.

Amen

But the fruit of the Spirit is love, joy, peace, patience, kindness, goodness, faith, gentleness, self-control. Against such things there is no law.

Galatians 5:22-23 HCSB

The next few days I am going to explore each fruit of the spirit. But get this, though this world hates God, it can not make any laws against His spirit. I mean nobody despises love, or joy, or peace, or any of the fruits of God's spirit, not even those who despise God. Why is that? Why is it that the world can deny God, but is unable to deny His character? It's because we were made in His image. Every person, believer or non believer, was made to exemplify the heart of God. We acknowledge God in our laws. We acknowledge Him in how we expect people to act. Our own right/wrong nature acknowledges that God is real. We can choose to ignore the existence of God all we want, but there is no way that we can deny the fruits of the spirit which are ingrained within us, and putting these fruits on display is one of the greatest ways we can use to point others to Jesus Christ.

Prayer:

God begin to work your fruit into my spirit. Over the next few days, show me your character and begin to lead me to walk in it. I pray that you would raise up love, joy, peace, patience, kindness, goodness, gentleness, and self control in my life as I grow closer to you.

Amen

But the fruit of the Spirit is love, joy, peace, patience, kindness, goodness, faith,

Galatians 5:22 HCSB

Love:

Paul said that the world will know we are Christ followers by our love. And Jesus said we must love our neighbors and our enemies. But what does Christlike love really look like? Is it brotherly love? Or the love we have for a good friend? Or a parent even? We know that it's not the way that the world sees love. But Paul tells us in Corinthians 13 that the greatest thing that remains throughout this life is love. Agape. The love of Jesus Christ that flows through us, into this world. The love of Jesus transforms. It transforms our hearts, and it transforms the hearts of those we love. And it's not always easy. It's no piece of cake for the king of the universe, the one who created everything and sits at the right hand of God, to leave His place in heaven in order to die for His enemies. But that is exactly what Jesus did for the glory of God. Christlike love is not tolerance. It's not making people feel comfortable, Jesus rarely did that. No, Christlike love is pointing others to the glory of God. It's telling those who don't know about His grace and mercy. It's leading others who have never been to the foot of the cross. It's praying fervently for those who have harmed you the most, just like Jesus prayed for you when your sin nailed Him to that cross. Christlike love means that you are willing to give your life so that others may see the glory of God. It's far more than making others happy, it's bringing Jesus to those who need Him.

Prayer:

Lord lead me in love. Help me to develop a love that brings glory to you, and you alone. God show me a deeper love, and help me to walk in love the way that Jesus did. Give me a love for my neighbor, and a love for those who may seem unlovable.

Amen

But the fruit of the Spirit is love, joy, peace, patience, kindness, goodness, faith, gentleness, self-control. Against such things there is no law.

Galatians 5:22-23 HCSB

Joy:

Joy is a tough fruit of the spirit for me to wrap my mind around sometimes. After all, there are tons of people who always seem to be happy that don't know Jesus. There are plenty of people who don't know Christ who seem to have it all together and never get flustered. So what exactly is the joy of the Lord? How is it different from a good attitude in life. This is where we get this fruit of the spirit totally mixed up sometimes. We see the joy of the Lord as the ability to be happy, but it's so much more supernatural than that. The joy of the Lord is constant in even the most turbulent circumstances, and it goes deeper than happiness, it is the understanding that this world is passing and we are headed to a much better one. The joy of the Lord transcends death because, with Jesus, death is a joyous occasion. The joy of the Lord leads us to love our enemies and pray for those who persecute us because our happiness does not depend on this world or on man, but on the blood of Jesus Christ. The difference between a general happiness and the joy of the Lord is just that, the Lord. A joy that is rooted in the Word of God is impossible to ignore to the rest of the world.

Prayer:

Lord give me joy. Help me to have your joy even in the midst of the worst of times. Go I pray that as you continue to mold me you would place inside my heart the ability to see you in every circumstance and lead me to choose joy daily.

Amen

But the fruit of the Spirit is love, joy, peace, patience, kindness, goodness, faith, gentleness, self-control. Against such things there is no law.

Galatians 5:22-23 HCSB

Peace:

Peace that passes all understanding. Everyone searches for it. Some search in the bottom of a bottle, or in a syringe. Some search for it in the gym, or in a significant other. But we all want it, we all need peace. But there is only one place to find it. Sure, the things of this world may bring a form of peace for a little while. Drugs and alcohol make us forget. The gym produces endorphins. Relationships make us feel wanted. But only the cross provides peace that lasts forever. Only Jesus gives peace that never fades. It's impossible to find peace without Christ. In Jesus is a peace that calms every storm. In Him is the peace that passes all understanding. And this kind of peace makes people stare. When you show peace in the craziest of storms people want to know how. When you refuse to be shaken when your world seems to be crumbling people want to know what steadies you. You want to see people flock to you? Remain calm in the most turbulent of situations, they won't be able to stay away. And when they ask where this supernatural peace comes from, because they will, be ready with one word. Jesus.

Prayer:

God give me your peace. Help me to understand that, even when it seems impossible, your peace can hold me up. Help me to be so rooted in you that you are the first and only one that I run to in the good times or the bad. Help me God to remain in you and be held by you.

Amen

But the fruit of the Spirit is love, joy, peace, patience, kindness, goodness, faith, gentleness, self-control. Against such things there is no law.

Galatians 5:22-23 HCSB

Patience:

Today's fruit of the spirit is patience, and it scares me to write about it publicly. Because that means I have to live it out. Patience is hard. I'm one to get things done. If I want something to happen I get to work, get my hands dirty, and make it happen. But Christ commands His followers to have patience. To wait upon the Lord. But patience doesn't mean laziness. The hardest thing about being patient is that sometimes, no matter how hard we work, the Lord simply tells us to wait. Abraham was promised a son years before Isaac was born. But he wasn't called to just sit and wait, God led Abraham to build the foundation for the family that he would one day have. David was told he would be king years before he actually wore the crown. But his years spent running from Saul and building his band if mighty men taught him to lead and showed the people of Israel who he was as a leader. The patience that we exercise as Christ followers is a working patience and requires a total reliance on Jesus Christ. Even when nothing seems to be going right, seek the kingdom of God. Do His work. And trust that God is in total control. That's patience.

Prayer:

Lord I pray that I would be patient in you. Lead me not into laziness, but cause me to rest and wait when you lead me to. Lord I pray that you would continue to mold me and make me, and give me patience when I can't see it happening.

Amen

But the fruit of the Spirit is love, joy, peace, patience, kindness, goodness, faith, gentleness, self-control. Against such things there is no law.

Galatians 5:22-23 HCSB

Kindness:

Kindness is a vital tool in the life of a believer. Truth is terribly important, living life without the truth of the gospel is pointless. But truth without kindness does very little in evangelism and discipleship. But don't get mixed up, kindness without truth is worthless, it means nothing. The kindness of God includes both a kind and truthful spirit. But it's not easy to exhibit the kindness of God. The kindness of God is self sacrificing, long suffering, and takes everything that you have to give. Christ showed kindness to even the men who nailed Him to a cross, begging God to forgive them. God shows kindness to us each and every day, holding back the judgement that we deserve even when we spit in His face. The good Samaritan showed kindness to a man who would have gone out of his way to avoid even walking the same road. The kindness of God takes up it's cross daily, denies self, and treats even enemies with love. The truth of the word of God is the greatest meal we could serve to those starving for it's truth, and kindness is the plate it is served on.

Prayer:

God lead me to be kind. Make me like your son and teach me to show kindness even when others show me hate. God help me to present your truth in kindness and lead me to treat others as you have treated me.

Amen

But the fruit of the Spirit is love, joy, peace, patience, kindness, goodness, faith, gentleness, self-control. Against such things there is no law.

Galatians 5:22-23 HCSB

Goodness:

Well duh. It makes sense right? That goodness would be a fruit of the spirit. But how often we neglect this fruit. Sure, if you saw an old woman struggling to cross the street, most of us would stop to help. That's good. So what's so supernatural about being good? Well, when God made man he said that His creation was good. We were good the way He made us, perfect. But when the first man fell and brought sin into his heart that goodness was tainted. The heart became wicked above all else. We struggle to do good, expecting nothing in return. Even when we do good by our own power it's tainted by sin. But the Holy spirit is only good. The savior that lives within us and works through us is not tainted by the sin that marks everything we do on our own. The supernatural goodness of God does not live in our flesh, but in the spirit that lives inside of us. Think about David. When he was given the opportunity to kill Saul, by all human standards, he would have had every right. Nobody would have blamed him. Many would have said he had done the right thing. But not the Holy spirit. The Holy spirit told David there was another standard of goodness, God's standard, the perfect standard. It's this kind of goodness that points others to Jesus. The goodness that causes us to love our enemies. The goodness that led David to mourn over the eventual death of Saul. The goodness that keeps us from getting even, or sacrificing integrity to get ahead. Let the goodness of God be the fruit you bear, and let it point others to Jesus Christ, the source of that goodness.

Prayer:

God you made me to be good in you. Help me to lean towards the goodness that you have called me to. Raise up your goodness in my heart and lead me to look more like Jesus each day.

Amen

But the fruit of the Spirit is love, joy, peace, patience, kindness, goodness, faith, gentleness, self-control. Against such things there is no law.

Galatians 5:22-23 HCSB

Faith:

Without faith it is impossible to please God. Without faith it's impossible to follow God's direction. We know what faith looks like, but why should we put our complete and total faith in Jesus Christ? Some people would say the only person you should put your faith in is you. But let's take a look at that idea for a second. I'm 5'7", 140 pounds on a heavy day. I have pretty average intelligence and a pretty good work ethic. I make pretty good decisions most of the time. I'm learning to be smart with my money. But I also know myself. I mess up. I say things I shouldn't, make boneheaded decisions, and am inclined to sin because of the flesh that I was born into. But God. God created the heavens and the Earth. He holds the entire universe in one hand without even thinking about it. When He speaks galaxies are born. The wind and waves listen to Him. And, while I treat my friends pretty good, Jesus died for me when I was His sworn enemy. He knows every second of the past, present, and future like the back of His hand. He is the sole owner of truth, peace, love, justice, and righteousness. There is nothing that can even begin to compare to Him. I'm not sure about you, but I would be far more willing to trust in what God can do than what I can do. He's got me beat by long shot. God deserves our faith. He has proven that over and over throughout all of time and before.

Prayer:

God grant me faith. Teach me to rely on you, not to lean on my own understanding. Show me that it is better to trust in you and you alone, and lead me to look to you each day.

Amen

But the fruit of the Spirit is love, joy, peace, patience, kindness, goodness, faith, gentleness, self-control. Against such things there is no law.

Galatians 5:22-23 HCSB

Gentleness:

Gentleness is one of my favorite fruits if the spirit. It's not one we would think of immediately when we think about what it means to be a Christ follower, but it is absolutely an important attribute of Jesus Christ. The ability to be strong AND gentle is a good sign of a great man. David could kill a thousand men in battle, but he could sit down and write some of the sweetest poems. Jesus was zealous enough to drive hustlers out of the temple with a whip, but gentle enough to lift a shamed woman to her feet after protecting her life from the religious leaders of the day. God is strong enough to send a world wide flood, or smite the entire Earth with fire, but gentle enough to send His son as the propitiation for the sins of the world. Never confuse gentleness with weakness. Show gentleness to people daily. Love your neighbor as your self. This is what it looks like to follow Jesus.

Prayer:

God make me gentle. Show me what it means to live for you and love those around me. Teach me to see the beauty of creation and the wonder of all that you have done. God teach me never to be proud, and show me the importance of a gentle spirit.

Amen

But the fruit of the Spirit is love, joy, peace, patience, kindness, goodness, faith, gentleness, self-control. Against such things there is no law.

Galatians 5:22-23 HCSB

Self control:

One of the most important characteristics of a Christ follower, yet one of the hardest to master, is self control. In order to have self control we must die to our desires. It means giving up what you want in order to obtain what Christ wants for you. In a world that pushes you to do what feels good and follow your heart it's tough to master self control. But we must if we plan to follow Jesus Christ, and Jesus had some blunt ways of telling people. When one man exclaimed that he wanted to follow Him Jesus said, "foxes have dens and birds have nests but the Son of Man has no place to lay His head." That doesn't sound like a self serving life. That sounds like a life of denying self for the furthering of the kingdom. I don't think this means that were not following Christ if we live in a house, but I do think it means we will be called to give up what makes us comfortable with our flesh and pick up our cross daily. And it's not just about sin. We exhibit self control in our spending habits (ouch) and the way we drive (road rage isn't becoming). We exhibit self control in how hard we work, even on the days it seems your boss doesn't understand what a valuable asset you are to their company. And we exhibit self control in our speech, especially when we are angry. It's hard sometimes, but there is no compromise, if you are not willing to die to yourself you can not follow Jesus Christ.

Prayer:

God I pray that you would lead me in each of the fruits of the spirit. Draw me closer to Jesus Christ with each passing day and help me to bring my self under your control each morning. Lead me to look more like Jesus so that others will see you in me.

Amen

When there are many words, sin is unavoidable, but the one who controls his lips is wise.

Proverbs 10:19 HCSB

There is so much in the Bible about controlling the tongue. James wrote about it, Paul warned about it. Solomon had much to say about it. Basically, if you constantly run your mouth you're going to mess up. Knowing when to speak and when to keep quiet is extremely important, and also very hard to do. Control of the tongue is a great sign of a person's maturity, both spiritual and worldly maturity. Solomon said that even a fool can look wise if he simply doesn't speak. And Paul taught to be slow to speak and slow to anger. Jesus exemplified this kind of maturity as He was led to the slaughter and "opened not his mouth." A sure sign of a mature person is when they know when to speak and when to keep quiet. I know that I have put myself in many sticky positions because of an uncontrolled tongue. Learn to tame your tongue and self discipline in other areas of your life will be much easier.

Prayer:

Lord help me to be slow to speak and quick to listen to your instruction. As I begin to develop a desperation for Jesus Christ I pray that you would lead me to bring this body under control and submit my heart and my tongue to you each day.

Amen

The boundary lines have fallen for me in pleasant places; indeed, I have a beautiful inheritance. I will praise the Lord who counsels me — even at night my conscience instructs me.

Psalms 16:6-7 HCSB

The Lord knows the plans He has for you. Plans to lead you closer and closer to Him each day. God has seen every moment of your life, from the past present and future. Why wouldn't you follow the one who knows exactly what lays in store for you. So often we view the commands of God as just a list of rules, and God as this angry figure who's waiting to strike you down if you don't follow them. But what if the commands of God lead us to the most pleasant life possible? What if following the commands of God is the best way for us to live the greatest life possible. It's true that following the commands of the Lord will lead you through the greatest life you could possibly have, and straying from the will of God always leads to strife. I praise God that He continues to lead me each day, even on the days when I turn to the left or to the right, His righteous hand is always there to prompt me into the most pleasant way imaginable.

Prayer:

God I thank you for the guideposts that you have placed in my life, and I ask you to forgive me for the many times I fail to follow them. Teach me to love your commands and to follow them so that I may run to you each day.

Amen

You have planted much but harvested little. You eat but never have enough to be satisfied. You drink but never have enough to become drunk. You put on clothes but never have enough to get warm. The wage earner puts his wages into a bag with a hole in it."

Haggai 1:6 HCSB

Anyone who works to establish a place in this world, while neglecting his relationship with Jesus Christ, works in vain. In the days of Haggai the Jews had decided to put off the building of the Lord's temple until they could establish their own kingdom. But the problem was that everything they did to establish themselves was useless because they had neglected the work the Lord had charged them with doing. If I work with diligence and build my body to be Mr. Olympia ready, but fail to work out my faith, any trophy I could earn would be in vain. Or if I work day in and day out until I sit on top of a multi-million dollar enterprise, but I neglect my relationship with Jesus Christ, I have done all that work to no avail. I would be pouring my pennies into a sack filled with holes, all of those achievements would be useless because my soul would be in disarray. But if I were to never achieve anything that this world sees as success, yet my spiritual life was in great shape, I would be as rich as a man could be. We ought to be pouring into our spiritual health twice as much as we do our physical. We ought to pour into our spiritual lives twice as much as we do our worldly successes because, if you were to lose everything but Jesus Christ you would have everything. But if you gain the whole world but lose your soul, you have lost eternal life. Devote yourself to the glory of God and you can not possibly lose.

Prayer:

God cause me to devote myself to growing closer to Jesus Christ. Remind me to work for your kingdom before trying to build mine. Show me that, without Jesus, I have gained nothing even with many successes.

Amen

So then, brothers, we are not obligated to the flesh to live according to the flesh, for if you live according to the flesh, you are going to die. But if by the Spirit you put to death the deeds of the body, you will live. All those led by God's Spirit are God's sons.

Romans 8:12-14 HCSB

Do not be deceived, faith without works is dead. James was adamant about living a life of righteousness. Many today proclaim salvation by faith, while neglecting holiness. This view of Christianity will lead many to the gates of hell. It is true that, in order to be saved all you must do is accept Jesus Christ as your Lord and savior. But if He is not your Lord then He is not your savior. A life that is saved by Jesus Christ will live for Jesus Christ. This does not mean that we are not afflicted by sin every single day, anyone who tries to tell you that he no longer sins is a liar and the truth is not in him. But if we allow sin to lord over our hearts then we can not be saved by Jesus Christ. We must not forget that God sent Jesus Christ to die on the cross because He must demand perfection and, though we will not attain it in this lifetime, we must pursue holiness as long as we dwell on this Earth. Salvation is free to all who will believe, but following Jesus will cost you all of yourself. We must crucify our flesh with Him, and be raised in the spirit every single day.

Prayer:

God help me to crucify my flesh today. Show me that faith without works is no faith at all, and lead me to walk in your ways rather than my own. God I need your spirit to lead and guide me, help me to listen when you speak and do as you have called me to do.

Amen

Brothers, I do not consider myself to have taken hold of it. But one thing I do: Forgetting what is behind and reaching forward to what is ahead, I pursue as my goal the prize promised by God's heavenly call in Christ Jesus.

Philippians 3:13-14 HCSB

We have the tendency to take Christianity and cheapen it to fit the way we want to live our lives. There are many Christians today who have accepted Jesus into their lives, go to church on Sundays, maybe even teach a Sunday school class, but are not chasing after Jesus Christ with all they have. I lived like this for a long time and , if I am not diligent, I slide right back into this sort of half-hearted Christianity. It's true that we ought not think too highly of ourselves, but we are children of God, called to pursue Him as we would the greatest of prizes imaginable. Don't fall into the trap of believing that claiming Jesus is enough. In fact Jesus said that many will call to Him on judgement day and He will have nothing to do with them because they did not know Him. No, our lives must be consumed with the prize which is a relationship with Jesus. It must be the loftiest goal in our hearts. We must train and study and fight to move closer to Him each day. It's true that our salvation belongs to Him alone, but we can't expect heaven without pursuing Jesus, and call ourselves true Christians. Pursue the goal, Jesus Christ, with all that you have today.

Prayer:

God I need your help in my pursuit of you. I have a tendency to walk towards the things of this world, help me to forsake all of it and run to you. Lead me to not only claim Jesus, but to pursue Him each day.

Amen

53

And make sure that there isn't any immoral or irreverent person like Esau, who sold his birthright in exchange for one meal. For you know that later, when he wanted to inherit the blessing, he was rejected because he didn't find any opportunity for repentance, though he sought it with tears.

Hebrews 12:16-17 HCSB

The Christian can not afford to neglect holiness in their life. Jesus absolutely accepts us as we are, but He doesn't leave us as we are. He changes and makes new our hearts until they bear His image. We as Christians are called to pursue holiness, to pursue the heart of Jesus Christ each day. Esau had the chance to inherit God's favor on him and all of his offspring, but he gave that up for a moment of gratification. Could you imagine trading a multi-million dollar Enterprise for a cup of soup? That would be insane. But when we trade holiness for the instant gratification of sin we are trading far more than all of the fortunes in the world put together. When we constantly pursue this world and the things that it offers we chase a perishable fortune, leaving behind an eternal inheritance. Many false teachers today will tell you that as long as you know Jesus you will go to heaven, but if your life doesn't reflect Jesus then you do not know Him. This doesn't mean that you won't mess up, or that you won't walk in the wrong direction for a time. But beware of a life that reflects this world while you claim Jesus Christ, because a life that does not reflect Jesus Christ does not belong to Him.

Prayer:

Lord I pray that when I look in the mirror I will see your son. Help me to reflect Jesus Christ over the ways of this world. I know that I stumble daily, help me to lift my eyes to you, get up, and walk in your ways.

Amen

Cast your burden on the Lord , and He will sustain you; He will never allow the righteous to be shaken.

Psalms 55:22 HCSB

Are you tired? Or broken? Or just having a hard time and don't know why? God cares. Peter wrote the same thing when he said to cast your cares upon the Lord, because He cares for you. As a Christian it is a guarantee that you will have trials of many kinds. Some days it will seem like the burdens just won't stop. Financial struggles, sickness, strained relationships, job loss, all of these things God cares about and won't let you be shaken by them. But that doesn't mean they won't rock your world. Some struggles you have will be life altering. But God will never give you a reason to doubt Him in the midst of the storm. Some burdens may leave you wondering if this is the end of it all, but God promises that, through Jesus, there is no end. God's love for you abounds and He knows every struggle and burden that will take its toll on you. But, through the blood of Jesus Christ, He has already sustained you through it all, all you have to do is trust that it's true.

Prayer:

God thank you for caring about me. Help me to cast all of my burdens on you. Show me that you love me and that you are able to sustain me, and help me to have the faith to believe it.

Amen

Now to Him who is able to do above and beyond all that we ask or think according to the power that works in us — to Him be glory in the church and in Christ Jesus to all generations, forever and ever. Amen.

Ephesians 3:20-21 HCSB

To God be the glory! That ought to be our cry, day in and day out, to God be all the glory! There is nothing on Earth or in heaven that compares to the glory of God, and there is certainly nothing more worth working for than the glory of God. Everything that we do, all that we say or think, the way we love others, all of it was meant for the glory of God. But get this! As often as I mess up, as many times as I fail daily, I can't mess up that glory. When we fail we don't even put a dent in God's glory, we're not that strong. What does happen when we fail to glorify God in our actions or speech is that we don't get to take part in His glorification in that scenario. All things that are meant for evil will be used for the glory of God, and all things good will glorify God. And you get to be a part of that glory, you get to work for His glory, if you only follow the plans that He has for you. So rest in the promise that Christianity isn't about you, it's about God's glory, and even though He doesn't need you He chose you to take part in His glorification through the blood of Jesus Christ.

Prayer:

God show me your glory. Thank you Lord for allowing me to live a life that glorifies me. Help me to live that way. I pray that when people look at me they see your glory above all else.

Amen

What is man that You remember him, the son of man that You look after him?

Psalms 8:4 HCSB

God doesn't owe me a thing, yet He gave me everything. The grace and mercy that God shows to each of us is completely unwarranted. We ask of Him answers that we don't deserve, we ask of Him favors that we could never repay. And yet He constantly pours out blessings on us that we don't deserve. Each breath is an undeserved mercy. Each day is a new chance that we could never earn. God's love for man is the greatest mystery in all of the universe, and yet He loves us. He knows exactly how many hairs are on your head, and how many are in your hairbrush at home. He knows how many times your heart has beat in your life, and how many times it will beat between now and the day you leave this life. God reaches out to touch your heart each and every day, often times only to be rejected by His own creation. It is impossible to understand the love of God, but it is a guarantee that He most certainly does love you, and will never stop.

Prayer:

God your love amazes me. Lead me to never stop being amazed by your love and grace towards me. Show my heart that you have a love for me, and for this world, that reaches far deeper than the depths of the ocean. Lead me each day towards your everlasting love and cause me not to forget you.

Amen

Therefore, if anyone is in Christ, he is a new creation; old things have passed away, and look, new things have come.

2 Corinthians 5:17 HCSB

Think about how awesome this promise is. When Christ enters our lives He doesn't just come in and clean us up. He doesn't demand that we make ourselves better before He will have anything to do with us. No, He comes in and transforms us. He creates in us a clean heart, and remakes us from the inside out. The moment you accept Jesus Christ as your Lord and savior the old man is dead, and a new man is created. So why don't we always act like it? Why do I have such a hard time being the new creation that Christ works in me? It's true that, when we are created anew by Jesus, the flesh wars even harder against the spirit that is within us, but I think that many times it is because I fail to trust that Jesus really has made me new. I mean, can He really get rid of the old me? The dirty sinful me? The short answer is yes, He can. And if you have accepted His free gift of grace He already has. But it is up to you to live out that new creation. To work out your own salvation. And to trust, daily, that you have a brand new heart, created in the image of the savior.

Prayer:

Create in me a clean heart oh God. Show me that you have made me new, and help me to walk in the newness that you have bestowed on me. Lead me each day to cast off the old and walk in the new that you have called me to walk in.

Amen

Brothers, do not grow weary in doing good.

2 Thessalonians 3:13 HCSB

There is so much depth in this little verse. Never grow weary in doing good, because doing good really can be tiring! In a world where the majority leans towards wickedness, where the path of least resistance is usually the wrong one, it's easy to get tired living a righteous life. The key is not to look within for the strength to do good. And it's definitely not to look to the world for the perseverance to press on in righteousness. The key is to rest in the spirit. To find your strength for good deeds in the Lord. To lean on Jesus Christ daily to energize you in your pursuit of holiness. The key is two fold. We ought to exhaust ourselves in living uprightly, and find the power to press on in the salvation and grace that is given liberally by God through Jesus. Deep study of the Word of God, and constant daily prayer are vital to making sure you don't grow weary in doing good. And, for the sake of those who are lost, please never let yourself grow weary of doing good.

Prayer:

God I need your strength to live worthy of the calling to which you have called me. Don't let me get tired of doing your will. Strengthen me each day and teach me to train my spirit towards the good that you have called me to.

Amen

A wise heart instructs its mouth and increases learning with its speech. Pleasant words are a honeycomb: sweet to the taste and health to the body.

Proverbs 16:23-24 HCSB

Be nice to each other. It sounds so simple, but it can be so hard to do sometimes. I don't know if it's because we feel the need to assert our dominance, or just because our hearts lean towards wickedness, but harsh words come out of our mouths way too easy some days. It doesn't seem like deep theology, but the way we speak to other people, people created in the image of God, truly reflects our relationship with Jesus Christ. Are your words uplifting? Encouraging? Caring? Or are they used to put others down so that you can stand a little higher? James spends a lot of time talking about taking the tongue. Most of the time we assume those verses are talking about cussing, but they speak just as much about how we speak to other people. Callous words come from a foolish heart. Remember that when you open your mouth to speak.

Prayer:

God teach me to speak only your words. Let the words that come from my mouth be uplifting and encouraging. Help me to treat others as your creation, made I n your image. Lord show me that you love those around me and help me to love those around me as well.

Amen

Don't let your spirit rush to be angry, for anger abides in the heart of fools.

Ecclesiastes 7:9 HCSB

Does your spirit rush to be angry? I know mine used to. I've heard, and said, things like "I go to the gym to protect other people" or "if I didn't work out I'd be mad all the time". That's what it looks like for anger to abide in your heart. It used to in mine for sure. I'd get fired up at the smallest things. But Solomon, the wisest man who ever lived, said that was foolish. It's foolish because unbridled anger clouds wisdom. You ever hit anything that your knuckles regretted immediately? Or said something that you wished you could take back? This doesn't mean that anger is always bad. Jesus got angry over things that He needed to get angry about. But anger did not abide in His heart, and it shouldn't abide in yours. An angry spirit constantly needs an outlet for its anger, be it the gym, or an addiction, or unrighteous behavior. But the spirit of the Lord keeps unbridled anger at bay, and brings up anger in the heart when it is needed. A spirit of anger always hurts most the person who has the angry spirit, not the people who that person shows anger towards. It's okay to get angry when it's needed, but don't allow anger to dwell in your heart. That's the difference between wise and foolish anger.

Prayer:

Lord teach me not to be an angry person. Help me God to lean on you when I feel anger welling up inside me and show me how to cast out anger when it seeks to cloud my judgement. Make me angry for the things that I need to be angry towards, and teach me to have a spirit that follows after you.

Amen

When He had come to the other side, to the region of the Gadarenes, two demon-possessed men met Him as they came out of the tombs. They were so violent that no one could pass that way. Suddenly they shouted, "What do You have to do with us, Son of God? Have You come here to torment us before the time? "

Matthew 8:28-29 HCSB

Think about the absolute power of Jesus Christ. Here He had just finished calming a raging storm with only words, and now even the demons are trembling at the mere sight of Him. Check this out! Jesus hops off of the boat with His disciples and comes across two demon possessed men. These demons were so bad that people would walk out of their way to make sure they didn't come across these men. Jesus steps off the boat and these demons freak out. He didn't even say anything! He just showed up and these nasty demons knew exactly what was fixing to go down. I mean, even the nastiest of demons simply beg Jesus to leave them alone. "let us just go somewhere else" they said. "send us to possess those pigs". They just wanted to get out of the presence of the son of God. This is the savior we serve. This is the spirit who lives inside of those who believe. He doesn't even have to lift a finger and the demons tremble. Satan already knows the war is over. The savior of the world is all powerful, and in control at all times. This is my Jesus. This is my savior. Is He yours?

Prayer:

Lord show me how magnificent you are and don't allow mw to forget that even the demons answer to you. God teach me to revere you each day and remind me that nothing exists outside of your control.

Amen

When Jesus had finished this sermon, the crowds were astonished at His teaching, because He was teaching them like one who had authority, and not like their scribes.

Matthew 7:28-29 HCSB

When Jesus spoke the authority of God was always evident in His words. When He performed miracles, forgave sins, taught His disciples, and sent them out to seek out the lost, He always did so with the authority of God. Why? Because He is God. Every word that Jesus spoke, every act He performed came directly from the Father. See, the Word was in the beginning. The Word was with God and the Word was God. When the time came the Word, Jesus Christ, became flesh and dwelt among men. He preached. He taught. He performed miracles. And He speaks to us today through His Holy and living Word. The Bible. That's right! The Bible has complete authority over your life. The Word of God, the Logos, the eternal word of life, has authority over this entire Earth. Whether we choose to submit, or to reject the Word of God, the Bible holds total authority over each and every one of us. Man can try to take authority over you, Satan will try to take authority over you, you can try to take authority over you, but the only true authority belongs to Jesus. Submit to Him, submit to His word, and the freedom that only He can give will be yours!

Prayer:

Lord thank you for sending your son. Cause me to submit to your control each day as I strive to draw closer to you. Remind me of the power of scripture and let your word be a lamp for my feet and a light for my path.

Amen

Though a righteous man falls seven times, he will get up, but the wicked will stumble into ruin.

Proverbs 24:16 HCSB

I've been there. It's easy to fall into sin and think, "well I'm already dirty" or "there is no way I can come back from this one". It's so easy to think that you will never escape the sin and shame that bind you. But you're wrong. It's true you will fail many times over your life, you will probably feel like you fail more often than you succeed, and some days that may even be true. But every time you get up and move forward, towards Jesus, you have won another battle against sin and shame. The devil knows that the only way he can win is to keep you down. Let him know that Jesus has already won and get up each time, moving towards the savior, always growing bigger, stronger, and better in your walk with Christ.

Prayer:

Lord I fail all the time. Some days I feel like I have fallen so far that you could never draw me back to you. God don't leave me in the midst of my sin and shame. Show me how to get back up when I fail. God make me aware of my shortcomings, and lead me to move one step closer to you each time I fail. Let me learn from my failures and continue to be formed to the image of Jesus.

Amen

"This is why I tell you: Don't worry about your life, what you will eat or what you will drink; or about your body, what you will wear. Isn't life more than food and the body more than clothing? But seek first the kingdom of God and His righteousness, and all these things will be provided for you.

Matthew 6:25, 33 HCSB

There is nothing more important than God. Not survival, not your family, not your friends, your job, fitness, nothing. Without God none of these things would matter because all of it would cease to exist without Him. This is why we should not worry. Not because God is going to drop a million dollars on you if you pray hard enough, or because we will never have hard times once we are saved, but because God is. If you seek with all your heart the one thing that remains for all eternity, the kingdom of God, then everything else will fall into place. It may not feel like it some days. It may feel like you are being crushed under the weight of responsibility, or it may feel like there is no way that you'll make it through the end of the day, but God has never failed and He never will. But if you seek to make it on your own, if you seek to gain the world at all costs, you will most certainly fail because you are broken. Seek what is whole. Seek what is true. Seek ye first the kingdom of God and life will take care of itself. Don't think of this as an excuse for laziness, but a promise that your work will be fruitful if it is in pursuit of the kingdom of the One True King.

Prayer:

Lord set my eyes upon you and your kingdom. I pray that I would not become so distracted by my worry that I seek anything outside of your will. Remind me God that your timing is perfect and your will towards me is good.

Amen

But we encourage you, brothers, to do so even more, to seek to lead a quiet life, to mind your own business, and to work with your own hands, as we commanded you, so that you may walk properly in the presence of outsiders and not be dependent on anyone.

1 Thessalonians 4:10-12 HCSB

How often we expect the Christian walk to be this great mountain top experience. We expect things to always be moving, choices to be clear, Miracles to be huge, basically we expect life to be epic. And in a way it is. But the true test of a Christian is this, how do you walk in the mundane? When life is quiet, and it seems God has stopped moving, do you still trust Him? Do you still follow Christ when it seems that you are heading down the mountain? There are many times like this in life. You're not in the valley, life really isn't that hard, but you're certainly not on the mountain top. Life just seems quiet, or maybe God seems quiet. Many times this is because God has you right where you need to be, and the path you're walking doesn't require any major movements. It is in these times that it is so important we seek the Lord and continue to do His work with vigor, because it's easy to lose that vigor when there is nothing to shake things up a bit. Maybe you're in this time right now, good! Paul says to seek to live a quiet life. Don't look at what your neighbor has going on and try to strive for that. Don't hunt for the next mountain top and let the time your spending in the quiet go to waste. Get to work, keep your eyes on Jesus, and praise God for where you are in your walk, and where He is taking you because, believe me, God's glory is the epic part.

Prayer:

Lord help me to be content in all of my circumstances. Help me Lord to look to you whether I am on the mountain top, in the valley, or somewhere in between. Teach me to be still and know that you are God.

Amen

Because of the Lord 's faithful love we do not perish, for His mercies never end. They are new every morning; great is Your faithfulness!

Lamentations 3:22-23 HCSB

It is the breath of God that swells your lungs so that you can breathe. It is the mercy of God that keeps us from the hell which we deserve. Without the hand of God this world would crumble to pieces, our lives would be exactly what the writer of Ecclesiastes describes in most of his book. Hell would be our only destination, no hope, no future, no meaning. But praise God His mercies never end! Each morning God breathes breath into your lungs and purpose into your life. Each morning God extends the blood of Jesus to wash away all of your sin and cleanse you from all unrighteousness. Nothing you have done warrants such mercy, in fact, everything you have done warrants the exact opposite. But God saw fit to send His son to die on the cross in order that His mercies could be extended to you each and every day. Blessed are those who understand their desperate need for Jesus, and for the tender mercies of God which give us life.

Prayer:

Lord show me my need for you. Remind me that apart from you nothing would exist. And lead me God to be thankful each day for your tender love and mercy. Make me desperate for you Lord.

Amen

How happy is the man who does not follow the advice of the wicked or take the path of sinners or join a group of mockers! Instead, his delight is in the Lord 's instruction, and he meditates on it day and night.

Psalms 1:1-2 HCSB

The first verse of the first Psalm is so important. The world will try to tell you how you should live and what you should believe. "love is love" "do what feels good" "the Bible is outdated." All of these, and more, are things we hear on a daily basis. But anything that does not line up with the word of God is a lie. A life led by the lies of this world leads to unhappiness because we are not made for this world, we are made for heaven, we were made for a relationship with God. I have always noticed that when I am stuck in sin nothing seems right. Even when I do good it feels wrong. I have listened to the lies of this world, and followed those lies many times, and they have always sucked the joy right out. But the way of the Lord is Joy filled and fulfilling. Follow the Word, meditate on it, let it permeate your heart, and the joy of the Lord will fill you until you overflow.

Prayer:

God let your joy be my strength. Lead me away from the traps that wicked people set before me and cause me to follow you each and every day. Lord let my joy be found in obedience to you.

Amen

For it is written: As I live, says the Lord, every knee will bow to Me, and every tongue will give praise to God.

Romans 14:11 HCSB

One day every knee will bow before God, and every tongue will confess, that Jesus Christ is Lord. It's a guarantee. There is no maybe, no "if/then" statement. Every person who has lived, is living, and will live will know without a doubt that Christ is king. But at that point it will be too late for those who refused to believe. When Jesus comes on the clouds and shows all that He is Lord, there will be no turning back from the decisions we have made concerning Him. If we know Christ this is the reason why we must be diligent in making disciples. Christ could come at any moment, and it would be too late for those who don't know Him. Too often we treat the lost as if we have all the time in the world to reach them, but our time is dwindling quickly. The peace and joy that Jesus provides will no longer be on the market when the whole world hits its knees. Do you live like that is reality? Do you minister as Jesus has called you to? If you don't know Jesus Christ as your Lord and savior, know that He offers life abundant right now. There is no time to waste in coming to Jesus Christ. Don't be fooled by this world, we will all bow to Him one day, but it will be a far more beautiful scene if you are Saved and sealed by Him.

Prayer:

God remind me each day of your coming return. Show me the urgency of the gospel Lord and lead me to point everyone I meet towards you. Thank you Lord that you are returning for me. Cause me to look forward and work as if you are coming soon.

Amen

But it is from Him that you are in Christ Jesus, who became God-given wisdom for us — our righteousness, sanctification, and redemption, in order that, as it is written: The one who boasts must boast in the Lord.

1 Corinthians 1:30-31 HCSB

The gospel, as simple as it is, can be tough for us to understand, especially if we try to look at it with human wisdom. Jesus, the son of God, had never known pain, sorrow, suffering, or temptation. And yet He gave all of that up to come and be humiliated, mutilated, and murdered for the sake of His enemies (you and me). Even while we despised Him, He loved us. Even while we spit on Him, and nailed His hands to the cross He forgave us. So how could I boast except for in His love? I have not been good enough to reach God. I could never be strong enough to climb to where He is. No amount of work that I do could ever qualify me to stand in the presence of God. But the cross has bridged the gap. Jesus has made the only way for us, prodigals all, to be reconciled to the father. Jesus I need thee, oh I need thee, every hour I need thee. No strength, no goodness, no works, no penance, guilt, or shame, could ever lead me into the arms of God. But you, oh Jesus, I will boast in what you have done for me.

Prayer:

God thank you for Jesus. Remind me of my shortcomings Lord and teach my heart the love of the savior for me.

Amen

Be gracious to me, God, according to Your faithful love; according to Your abundant compassion, blot out my rebellion.

Psalms 51:1 HCSB

No amount of penance, good works, or elaborate prayer can cleanse you from your sin. Trust me, I need the forgiveness of Jesus every single day. But if I seek to earn the forgiveness of God, or I do good works out of a want for God's forgiveness or good will, then I have fallen way off track. Forgiveness is found in Jesus Christ, and Jesus Christ alone, and is born of the grace and mercy of God. Know that you never deserved the forgiveness and salvation given by God, so why do we try to work so hard to earn it after we have been saved? Don't get me wrong, we were created to do good works, good works which were prepared in advance for us to do. But these works can never earn us the forgiveness that we need. So many work tirelessly to earn God's grace, when we ought to be working tirelessly to glorify God because of the grace that has already been given to us. Isn't that a weight off your shoulders? I know it is off mine. If I had to work for God's forgiveness, I would be working 24 hours a day and it still wouldn't be enough. No, the forgiveness is already there, all we must do is step into it humbly, and ask God to speak into our hearts what He has already done.

Prayer:

Be gracious to me God because of your son. Thank you for your tender love and mercy. Help me God to rest in your forgiveness, and work for your glory alone.

Amen

but honor the Messiah as Lord in your hearts. Always be ready to give a defense to anyone who asks you for a reason for the hope that is in you.

1 Peter 3:15 HCSB

How big is Jesus in your life? If someone were to ask you why you love Jesus so much would you know exactly what to say? Me? I love Jesus because He daily changes my heart. I grow closer to Him and then I mess up. Then I turn and grow closer to Him and then I mess up. Over and over again I constantly feel like I've let Jesus down for the last time. I'm not organized, I forget things that are important, I sin on the daily, I fail my wife, I fail my friends, I fail my family, and I fail God. And yet, Jesus saves me every single day. Jesus Christ has spoken to my heart and drawn me closer to Him more times than I can count. My point is, I love Jesus so much because He won't let me stop. Every day of my life has been a reminder of the fact that He has never given up on me. That He loves me. That He pursues me. So why do you love Jesus so much? What would you say if I asked you that question? Is He so big in your life that you already have that answer constantly on your heart? Think about all that He has done for you, I think you'll find that it will touch your heart.

Prayer:

God thank you for caring for me even before I cared for you. Help me to always be ready to give an answer when people ask why I love you so much. Lord make me bold in proclaiming my faith, and humble in recognizing how deep your love is for me.

Amen

And don't grieve God's Holy Spirit. You were sealed by Him for the day of redemption. All bitterness, anger and wrath, shouting and slander must be removed from you, along with all malice. And be kind and compassionate to one another, forgiving one another, just as God also forgave you in Christ.

Ephesians 4:30-32 HCSB

Forgiveness is the greatest thing we ever received, and the greatest thing we can ever give. When we as Christians bicker amongst ourselves, hold grudges, spread rumors, and refuse to forgive our brothers and sisters in Christ, we grieve the Holy spirit. Bitterness, anger, slander, unforgiveness, these things have no place in the heart of the believer. Christians ought to be the most unified group of people on this planet. We all have one heavenly father who is above all, through all, and in all of us. We have the most unifying father in the universe. All of us as Christians are sinners, once enemies of God, and we have all been extended an infinite amount of forgiveness by the father. We must extend the same to our brothers and sisters in Christ, we must join together and be of one mind; the mind of our Lord and savior Jesus Christ. Forgive one another, ask for forgiveness from one another, and seek to be unified with one another. That is one of the greatest marks of the Christian.

Prayer:

Lord thank you for the family that I have been adopted into through the blood of Jesus, your son. God I lift up the unity of the church. Help us to be of one mind, because we have one savior. Help me Lord to love my brothers and sisters and honor them as you would have me to.

Amen

Then he said to them, "Go and eat what is rich, drink what is sweet, and send portions to those who have nothing prepared, since today is holy to our Lord. Do not grieve, because the joy of the Lord is your stronghold."

Nehemiah 8:10 HCSB

The joy of the Lord is my strength. Not how much I can bench press, or what kind of car I own, or the job that I have. The strength that I have through the joy that is in my heart is the greatest strength I could ever be endowed with. But what was going on here in this passage? Where does the joy of the Lord come from? How do we get it? Of course, the salvation offered through Jesus is the greatest joy in heaven and on Earth, but if I don't actively seek Him how could I ever experience this joy in this life? See in this passage of Nehemiah the Jewish people had just gathered in the town square for the reading of the Word of God. They had gathered to listen to the law of the Lord, and we're finding Joy in the Words of their Lord. They were delighting in God's word. Do you delight in God's word? Do you leave church on Sunday thankful that the Lord chose to speak to you through His word? Do you open your Bible in anticipation, knowing that God will still your heart and impart His joy in your life through His words? The Jewish people were so glad to hear God's word in this passage because they had been kept from doing so for years while in exile. It was music to their ears to finally hear, once again, the promises and commands of God. Let a delight in God's word take hold of your heart today, and let the Joy of the Lord strengthen you.

Prayer:

God let the joy that comes from you be my strength. Give me a delight for your word. Help me God to love scripture the way that David loved your words. Let my heart be glad each day that I get to hear from you, and give me a hunger for the Bible.

Amen

If you remain in Me and My words remain in you, ask whatever you want and it will be done for you. My Father is glorified by this: that you produce much fruit and prove to be My disciples.

John 15:7-8 HCSB

When it comes to taking verses out of context, we tend to do it to this one all the time. Many times we as Christians have used this verse to make ourselves believe that Jesus will do anything we pray for as long as we believe hard enough. But these two verses have a far deeper, and more beautiful meaning than just that. We assume that the promise here is that we will get everything if we only believe in Jesus enough. But these verses are a much better promise, a promise that Jesus will change our hearts to look more and more like Him each day. Jesus said here, "if you remain in me, and my words in you THEN ask whatever you want and it will be done for you." See, when we persevere in Christ, and His word remains in our hearts, our hearts begin to look more and more like His. Our will begins to align with the will of Jesus. And when our will aligns with the will of Jesus, then the things we ask of Him will be His will. Remember when Christ prayed for Himself in the garden of Gethsemane. He asked God for His will to be done, leading Him to the cross and to your salvation, and most importantly, God's glory. Remain in Christ, seek to glorify God in all that you do, and anything you ask will be done, because it will be God's will.

Prayer:

God make me according to your will. I pray that, as I grow closer to you each day, that your will might begin to become my will. God teach me to want all that you want, and to do all that you have called me to do.

Amen

For we do not have an enduring city here; instead, we seek the one to come.

Hebrews 13:14 HCSB

Do you ever feel like you don't belong? Do you feel like you just don't fit in here sometimes? That's probably because you weren't made for this world. Your heart was built for heaven. You were made to live in the everlasting light of God's love. Whether you have accepted Jesus Christ or not, you were not meant to make a home here in this broken world. Your heart is yearning for heaven. It's yearning to be in the presence of God. That's why we get so restless here. It's why we are plagued with wondering if we are where we belong, or doing what we are meant to do. As long as you seek your home in this world you will always yearning for a new home, a different place. The grass will always be greener, no matter where you go, because this world is temporary. But Heaven is eternal. It's real. And it's waiting for you to come home again. If you know Christ as your Lord and savior a place is already prepared for you in Heaven, all you're doing here is travelling home, and bringing as many people with you as you can. Don't get caught up in trying to belong here. It won't work. Your heart will never fit with this world. Instead, look up to the place that was meant to be your everlasting dwelling place, and the savior who longs to take you there.

Prayer:

God I long for heaven. I pray that you would continue to remind me that I do not belong to this world. Make my heart ready to be home, and eager to bring as many with me as will come.

Amen

Remain in Me, and I in you. Just as a branch is unable to produce fruit by itself unless it remains on the vine, so neither can you unless you remain in Me. "I am the vine; you are the branches. The one who remains in Me and I in him produces much fruit, because you can do nothing without Me.

John 15:4-5 HCSB

Don't get caught up in trying to do good on your own power. It just doesn't work. This is why desperation for Jesus is so vitally important, because we must grow from Him, not try to grow towards Him. Jesus must be your vine. Your entire life must stem from His tender love and mercy. There is a reason that Isaiah said that our righteousness is as filthy rags, and it's not because we are useless or unable to perform any good works. Think about an old oily rag. If you try to use one to clean up a mess, what happens? It just spreads the mess around, leaving it just as bad as when you started. But take that oily rag and clean it, make it look brand new, and it cleans like a charm. It's the same for us. When I try to do good of my own power it usually comes out just as bad, or worse, in the end. It's because I am tainted. My heart, separate from the vine, is oily. But when your heart stems from Jesus Christ, not only are you made clean, you are daily made new. Under the blood you are a new rag every day. That means when your good works stem from the tender love and mercy of Jesus, they always do good. Stop trying to work FOR Jesus, and begin working FROM Jesus.

Prayer:

Lord teach me to remain in you. Remind me God that it is not me who wills and works to do what is good, but your spirit in me. Teach me to work from Jesus Christ, in His power, rather than for Jesus Christ in my own limited power.

Amen

Love consists in this: not that we loved God, but that He loved us and sent His Son to be the propitiation for our sins.

1 John 4:10 HCSB

Love is not man made. Love was placed in us by God, and love is made stronger in us the closer we are to Jesus. The more you love God, the more you delight in His word and lean on His son, the better you are able to love others. One thing we must do is stop trying to love by our own power. I can't possibly give my wife the love that she deserves on my own. I could never show the love that the world needs unless it comes from God. And I certainly could never love my enemy by my own power. No, our love must come from the Lord. We ought to be on our knees daily, asking God to fill our hearts with His love so that it can pour out of us to those around us. So that we can lift others up and point all who know us to the son of God. God loves you. He loved you when you were still His enemy. He loves you so passionately that He sent His son to be tortured and killed on a cross for you. Don't allow this world to define love for you, because it will always be wrong. Instead look to the origin of love, the One who is love. And allow Him to fill you with His love so that you can pour it out to those around you.

Prayer:

Lord teach me your love. Help me God to love, not only those around me who love me, but my enemy as you have loved me. Continue Lord to cause your love to flow through me, to others. And lead me to be your hands and feet.

Amen

Jesus responded, "I assure you: Everyone who commits sin is a slave of sin. A slave does not remain in the household forever, but a son does remain forever. Therefore, if the Son sets you free, you really will be free.

John 8:34-36 HCSB

The day that Jesus walked out of the grave and declared that anyone He sets free is truly free from sin, that is the greatest Independence day in history. Because He has set us free, we can stand at the foot of the throne of judgement, unashamed, because His blood covers all of our transgressions. Through His declaration of our Independence we are made children of God! Have you tasted that freedom today? Is your life free from the bondage of sin and shame? If it is, rejoice every day, because Christ has broken the chains of the flesh that held your heart. You are truly free. If you have yet to taste the freedom that Jesus Christ brings, lift up your shackles to Him and allow His blood to break right through them. Because living in a country that is free, but still being held by the shackles of sin and shame, is no freedom at all.

Prayer:

God set me free from the sin that so easily ensnares me. Help me Lord to live in the freedom that your son died to bring to me. Remind me that I am free indeed and that Jesus came to bring life that is abundant and free. Remind me Lord of just how much has been given to me.

Amen

To the pure, everything is pure, but to those who are defiled and unbelieving nothing is pure; in fact, both their mind and conscience are defiled. They profess to know God, but they deny Him by their works. They are detestable, disobedient, and disqualified for any good work.

Titus 1:15-16 HCSB

This is why we as Christians must strive for purity. Crete was full of people who professed to be Christians, but refused to live the way Christ had called them to. Because of this, the work of God was not being done in Crete. See, when we chase after things that are not of God, our goals and ambitions can not line up with God's plan. What happens then is, we begin to fool ourselves into believing that we are doing "good enough for God, when in reality we are working directly against Him. So the next time that someone tries to make you feel like you are self-righteous for believing that we ought to live the way Jesus called us to, or someone tries to tell you that the commands of the Bible are for some but not all, just remember that those who love Jesus love His work. And if we don't love His work, we ought to ask Him to take a look at our hearts and reveal to us where we have turned from Him.

Prayer:

Lord help me to love your word, your work, and your commands. Teach me God that you know what is best for me, and that I am called to live worthy of the calling you have placed on my life. Forgive me when I fall short and lead me in the way of everlasting.

Amen

"If you know Me, you will also know My Father. From now on you do know Him and have seen Him." "Lord," said Philip, "show us the Father, and that's enough for us." Jesus said to him, "Have I been among you all this time without your knowing Me, Philip? The one who has seen Me has seen the Father. How can you say, 'Show us the Father'?

John 14:7-9 HCSB

Raise your hand if you tend to be a Phillip. I find myself often standing in the presence of Jesus, asking Him to show Himself to me. It's the flesh. Our flesh is always trying to overshadow the presence of God in our lives. Jesus had just told the disciples, blatantly I might add, that He was God. And yet they still had a hard time figuring it out. And that's okay. It's okay if you're not really feeling God's presence today, because He is still there. It's okay if you feel like your prayers just aren't reaching His ears, because they truly are. It's okay if you feel tired, broken, or like you just can't go any farther, because you are currently being held by God. You're not always going to feel God. You're not always going to see Him when He is standing right in front of you, because the flesh is always battling within you. I find that, in these moments, it is best to just say "Jesus I don't feel you here". Be honest with the Lord, and be honest with yourself. Because in that moment of honesty Jesus will reveal Himself to you. He is always faithful, even when you are faithless. He is always there, even when your flesh won't let you see Him. And He is always pursuing your heart, even when you think you have run as far as you can from Him. If you feel like God is not present with you today, ask Jesus to reveal Himself to you right now and, gently, quietly, He will.

Prayer:

Jesus open my eyes to see you. Remind me that you are always with me, and show me once again how much you love me. Forgive me for looking past you at this world sometimes, and show me that I am never outside of your presence.

Amen

When all has been heard, the conclusion of the matter is: fear God and keep His commands, because this is for all humanity. For God will bring every act to judgment, including every hidden thing, whether good or evil.

Ecclesiastes 12:13-14 HCSB

I feel like the writer of Ecclesiastes a lot more than I'd like to admit to myself sometimes. Life tends to feel a lot like running on a treadmill; you get tired but you really don't go anywhere. This is what Solomon was dealing with throughout the book of Ecclesiastes. Life was looking bleak, tiring, meaningless. Except for one thing, God Almighty. Without God this world truly has no meaning. We live, and we die. Apart from God, nothing in between those two could possibly matter. In finding purpose in this life the best place to start is at the end of Ecclesiastes. You can learn everything there is to learn in this world. You can do everything there is to do, and be everything there is to be. At the end of it all, only God will still remain. See you can never find the end of God. You could search God for infinite lifetimes and never reach the end of His love, grace, peace, righteousness, etc. There is no end to the pursuit of God, and the search for His heart will fill you to the brim and keep you full. Don't get caught up in pursuing this world. It, and everything in it, will end. Pursue God, obey Him, and fear Him, because there is no end with God Almighty.

Prayer:

God I thank you that you are eternal. Help me Lord to turn my eyes away from the things of this world, and let them rest on your son Jesus. Remind me God that all of this world will end, but you remain forever.

Amen

Don't worry about anything, but in everything, through prayer and petition with thanksgiving, let your requests be made known to God. And the peace of God, which surpasses every thought, will guard your hearts and minds in Christ Jesus.

Philippians 4:6-7 HCSB

"In Christ Jesus". What a wonderful promise that God's word makes to us. If we remain in Christ Jesus, everything is taken care of. This doesn't mean that we will never have problems, or that everything will work out exactly the way we would like. But it does mean that, if we remain in Christ, our hearts will be comforted. Our minds can be at ease because of the blood of Jesus Christ. See, God wants to hear our requests. He wants to know what lays heavy on our hearts. And then, no matter the outcome, He will comfort us with His tender love and mercy, in Christ Jesus. Jesus is the key. Throughout the whole of the Bible, Jesus is the key. The Old Testament pointed to Christ. The old law showed us that it is impossible to live up to the standard that God must set. So there had to be a way for you and I to be restored, for the standard to be met. And so Christ was revealed in the New Testament. He fulfilled the law with His blood, and He offers peace because He justifies us, in Christ Jesus. We must become desperate for Jesus Christ. We must seek Him each and every day, understanding that there is never a moment when we don't need Him. We must live our lives in Christ Jesus, and the peace of God Almighty will overflow our hearts and minds.

Prayer:

God thank you for Jesus. I could never express just how much I need your son. Remind me each day to rest in Christ, and teach my heart of my desperate need for Him.

Amen

For I know the plans I have for you" — this is the Lord 's declaration — "plans for your welfare, not for disaster, to give you a future and a hope. You will call to Me and come and pray to Me, and I will listen to you. You will seek Me and find Me when you search for Me with all your heart.

Jeremiah 29:11-13 HCSB

This world is a sea of faces. There are so many people, past, present, and future, that there is no way that you can be important to God. Right? Wrong. We were created by a God who is mighty enough to care, not only for this entire world, but for your soul. God knows you. He knows how many hairs are on your head at any given moment. He even knows how many hairs are clinging to the bristles of the hairbrush on your bathroom sink! He knows what your heart needs right now. He knows how many steps you will take over the course of your life, and exactly where those steps will take you. He cares for you enough to have laid out a plan, before the foundations of the world we're even in place, a plan to lead you closer and closer to Him. He cares enough about you that, though you held the nails that fastened His son to the cross, He sent Christ to free you from your sin anyways. You are precious to God. Your life has purpose. It has meaning. It means something to the creator of the world. At any given point in time His thoughts towards you outnumber the grains of sand on the face of this Earth! God has a plan to care for your soul. Lean on that plan today. Accept it and allow your heart to be held by the one who holds the world.

Prayer:

God thank you for knowing me. Thank you for forming me long before I ever had breath in my lungs. Thank you for caring for me. Help me today to lean on you and the plans that you have for me.

Amen

For the mind-set of the flesh is death, but the mind-set of the Spirit is life and peace. For the mind-set of the flesh is hostile to God because it does not submit itself to God's law, for it is unable to do so. Those who are in the flesh cannot please God.

Romans 8:6-8 HCSB

You were born an enemy of God, contrary to His nature. God could not accept you in your flesh, it would be impossible for Him. But He did something. Something huge. Even while you were His enemy, He sent His son in the flesh, to destroy the flesh. Jesus Christ, who had only ever known life and peace, was sent into this world to endure and overcome the flesh so that you could be called a friend of God. Those of us who remain in the flesh can never please God. You can never be reconciled to the father and remain in the flesh. So, it is Jesus who enters into our lives, breaks the chains that the flesh has placed on our hearts, and releases the spirit in us to restore us unto God. We can never boast in our own righteousness because it does not exist within our flesh. But we can forever boast in Jesus Christ and the work that He has done in our hearts. What a joy it is to be loved by one you have hated. What a peace it is to be restored by the one you nailed to the cross. And what an abundant Life it is to stand unashamed at the foot of the throne of God because Jesus will be there saying "I have paid for this one". If you already know this peace, walk in it. Don't let your heart wander back to the chains of the flesh. And if you don't already know the peace that Jesus offers, there is a place at the table of grace with your name on it. Flee from the flesh, and run to Jesus today.

Prayer:

God you loved me when I set my heart against you. You saved me when I was your enemy. How awesome is your love for me God? I could never reach the end of your love in a thousand lifetimes. Remind me of how greatly I am loved by you today Lord.

Amen

For everyone who practices wicked things hates the light and avoids it, so that his deeds may not be exposed. But anyone who lives by the truth comes to the light, so that his works may be shown to be accomplished by God."

John 3:20-21 HCSB

Why do we hate the light when we sin? I don't know about you, but I've never thought "hey everyone is watching, I think I'm gonna do something I shouldn't". No, we always tend to hide our shortcomings. But this is not from God. When we hide our sin, especially when we are successful at doing so, the desire to continue in sin grows. We allow our flesh to become brave, to make us feel like it's possible to find worldly pleasure without anyone finding out. But this is a lie from the enemy. No, we can't hide in the darkness. We must refuse to seek shelter in the darkness of this world. Begin to spend time in the light. Pour out your sinfulness, first before the Lord and, if you need accountability, before another believer who can help you to grow towards Jesus. We can't hide our faults from God, but we can allow His light to illuminate our lives so that the whole world can see the work He has done in us.

Prayer:

God I pray that I never feel successful in hiding my sin. Bring the darkest parts of me to light Lord so that I can be transformed into the image of Jesus. Walk with me God and lead me to live in the light of your glory.

Amen

Consider it a great joy, my brothers, whenever you experience various trials, knowing that the testing of your faith produces endurance. But endurance must do its complete work, so that you may be mature and complete, lacking nothing.

James 1:2-4 HCSB

I think that one of the greatest marks of the Christian Life is endurance. But how do we do that? We hear it all the time. Endure, persevere, press on, move forward. But how do we do all of these things? I think that it's much simpler than we often try to make it. It's kind of like Nike says, "just do it". There's no magic formula to enduring. No twelve step program that can make it happen. It's just one step. Keep moving forward. Have you fallen into the trap of sin? Be like Peter, step forward and go feed the sheep of Jesus. Does it feel like the whole world is coming against you? Be like Paul and simply continue to follow Jesus and preach the gospel, even if it means something as dark as imprisonment. And the examples go on and on. John was exiled. James was ridiculed and martyred. Polycarp was burned at the stake. Martin Luther was excommunicated. Thousands of Christians in the middle East face the threat of death daily, and in China Christians must meet in secret. Honestly, the toughest challenge we face here in America right now is that people might not like us if we profess our faith. We must persevere. Our greatest example did. Christ was hung on a cross. He persevered for your heart. Press on and seek His heart. Don't give up. Seek wisdom. Seek Jesus. And seek the Lord.

Prayer:

God grant me the strength to press on in you. I need your guidance each and every day, Lord teach me how to move forward whatever my circumstances. Create in me a spirit of endurance Lord until the day that I am home with you.

Amen

You are my shelter and my shield; I put my hope in Your word. Depart from me, you evil ones, so that I may obey my God's commands.

Psalms 119:114-115 HCSB

I love psalm 119 because it's focus is on delighting in the word of God. Where do you run to for shelter? Is it a relationship? A secret sin? Work? The gym? Or is it into the arms of God almighty? Obedience to God is not only necessary for our growth in Jesus Christ, but for our shelter. The commands of God are meant to bless and keep you. Jeremiah 29:11 says that God has plans for you, not to harm you, but to make you prosperous spiritually. When you live in the shelter of God's word your heart is kept safe from sin, from shame, and guilt. You are led in the way of everlasting when you live under the shadow of His wings! Think about that. God doesn't just call you to obedience and then leave you on your own to follow Him. He provides the way, and the shelter along that way.

As much as I love the gym, there is no comparison between the temporary peace it provides and the everlasting protection of the Word of God. Where you run to for shelter and comfort matters and, if it's not into the shelter of God's word, it's only sub-par.

Prayer:

God lead me to you always. Help me Lord not to run to things that are temporary for shelter, but to Jesus who is everlasting. Create in me a love for your word and a desire to live in your commands Lord.

Amen

Go, therefore, and make disciples of all nations, baptizing them in the name of the Father and of the Son and of the Holy Spirit, teaching them to observe everything I have commanded you. And remember, I am with you always, to the end of the age."

Matthew 28:19-20 HCSB

Do you ever wonder if maybe people are right? That they're right when they tell you that you're closed minded? Or dogmatic? Or just too stuck on this whole Jesus thing? Maybe you feel like they are right when they say you just need to change the gospel to fit the times. That it doesn't work for modern society. Well don't worry. Jesus knew you would feel this way. He saw it coming, He sees everything coming. And He gave you directions on exactly what to do. He told us to go and make disciples of all nations. Go to work and make disciples. Go to school and make disciples. Go out into every place and make disciples. We are not meant to change the gospel so that others like it. We are not meant to open our minds to the doctrines of the world, except to understand how we can better take the Gospel to it. When people come against you, saying you're too preachy or closed minded, remember that Jesus Christ is with you through the rest of your life, pouring His gospel into your heart to be spread to the ends of the Earth.

Prayer:

God lead me to preach your gospel everywhere I go. Give me a boldness Lord to take the truth of your word as it is and spread it wherever I have an opportunity. I pray that I would not be changed by the world around me, but by your Word. I pray for the heart of each person I come in contact with, that they would be softened towards your word.

Amen

Search me, God, and know my heart; test me and know my concerns. See if there is any offensive way in me; lead me in the everlasting way.

Psalms 139:23-24 HCSB

I love this verse. David was a messed up dude. He made mistakes that would make the worst of sinners blush. But he always had his heart open before God. David lived broken before the Lord. Do you live broken before God? Are you willing to let your sin and shame spill out before God so that He can reach down and make you new? Try it. Pray this verse one time, and allow God to break your heart for what breaks His. We must come to the understanding of our own lostness before we can allow God to lead us in the way of everlasting, and we must remain aware of the flesh that lives within us. This doesn't mean that we wallow in our sin. No, David never did that. He looked past his sin, bare before God, and looked to the Lord for forgiveness and grace. When we become aware of our sin, our selfishness, our lust, our greed, all of the things within us that break the heart of God, and look to Him to lift us out of the mire, He will certainly lead us down the path of everlasting. Ask God to make you aware of your flesh today, and then ask Him to make you even more aware of Himself.

Prayer:

Search me God. Show me what is in my heart that hurts yours. Make me into a new creation today and lead me towards Jesus every day, as long as I am alive.

Amen